JavaScript for Sound Artists

Learn how to program JavaScript while creating interactive audio applications with *JavaScript for Sound Artists: Learn to Code with the Web Audio API*! William Turner and Steve Leonard showcase the basics of JavaScript language programming so that readers can learn how to build browser-based audio applications such as music synthesizers and drum machines. The companion website offers further opportunity for growth. Web Audio API instruction includes oscillators, audio file loading and playback, basic audio manipulation, panning, and time. This book encompasses all of the basic features of JavaScript with aspects of the Web Audio API to heighten the capability of any browser.

Key Features

- Uses the readers' existing knowledge of audio technology to facilitate learning how to program using JavaScript. The teaching will be done through a series of annotated examples and explanations.

- Downloadable code examples and links to additional reference material included on the book's companion website.

- This book makes learning programming more approachable to nonprofessional programmers.

The context of teaching JavaScript for the creative audio community in this manner does not exist anywhere else in the market and uses example-based teaching.

William Turner is a technical trainer with over 13 years of experience. He currently operates a boutique web development and training company at helpknow.com.

Steve Leonard is a technical writer for Juniper Networks and developed some of the initial documentation for the Cisco Nexus 7000 Series of switches among other products. He now writes the internal programmer guide for developers of Juniper's next-generation operating system and is responsible for the network management documentation for end users of that new OS.

JavaScript for

Sound Artists

Learn to Code with the Web Audio API

2nd Edition

Authored by: **William Turner**

Edited by: **Steve Leonard**

CRC Press
Taylor & Francis Group
Boca Raton London New York

CRC Press is an imprint of the
Taylor & Francis Group, an **informa** business

Second Edition published 2023
by CRC Press
6000 Broken Sound Parkway NW, Suite 300, Boca Raton, FL 33487-2742

and by CRC Press
4 Park Square, Milton Park, Abingdon, Oxon, OX14 4RN

CRC Press is an imprint of Taylor & Francis Group, LLC

© 2023 Taylor & Francis Group, LLC
First Edition published by CRC Press 2017

ISBN: 978-1-032-06273-0 (hbk)
ISBN: 978-1-032-06272-3 (pbk)
ISBN: 978-1-003-20149-6 (ebk)

DOI: 10.1201/9781003201496

Typeset in MinionPro
by codeMantra

Access the Support Material: https://www.routledge.com/9781032062723

This book is dedicated to the loving memory
of my mother, Bonnie Turner.

I want to thank the Littlejohn/Craft family. Maureen, you've
been like a second mother and I don't know what I'd do
without you. Gabe, you're going to be a great father!

I also want to thank Earl Jenkins, Steve Leonard,
and Meilin Obinata for caring enough to listen
when I needed someone to talk to. I love you all!

William Turner

Contents

3. Operators   27

4. Conditional Statements, Loops, and Scope   35

10. Simplifying DOM Programming with JQuery   II5

II. Loading and Playing Audio Files   I27

Preface

Learning to program can be daunting, and we want to be the first to congratulate you for taking on the challenge! Second, we want to thank you for choosing this book.

▮▮ Who Is This Book For?

This book is for anyone who is involved in the world of creative audio and wants to learn to program using the JavaScript language. There are many programming books directed toward artists to help them build websites, mobile applications, games, and other things, but next to none is directed exclusively toward the sound arts community. This book is designed to fill this role and to teach the fundamentals of web-based software development, and specifically, the basics of the JavaScript programming language to *sound artists*.

▮▮ What This Book Is *Not?*

This book is not an audio technology reference. It does not take the time to explain the fundamentals of audio theory or sound engineering in depth. Words and phrases like *dynamic range compression, convolution reverb, and sample rate* are thrown around like candy with only a cursory explanation (if they are explained at all). We assume that you are either familiar with many of these core audio concepts or know enough to find the answers on your own. If you need an accommodating audio technology reference, we suggest David Miles Huber's excellent book *Modern Recording Techniques*, Taylor & Francis.

> This book is also not directed toward experienced programmers who are simply interested in JavaScript or the Web Audio API. If this describes you, then you may find some value here, but you are not the intended audience.

▮ How to Learn to Program

The following are a few tips to help you get the most from this book.

Make Connections

Generally, it is easier to learn new things by making associations and connections to areas that you are already familiar with. If you have ever programmed a synth or a MIDI sequencer, then you have already done a *form* of programming. The contents of this book are designed to be a bridge that connects a world you are (presumably) familiar with (sound and audio technology) to a topic you are less familiar with—JavaScript and programming. We suggest that you tap into whatever has drawn you to sound art while learning the material in this book.

Flow and Frustration Are Not Opposites

It's very important to embrace a sense of flow when learning to program. It is also important to embrace frustration as *part of the flow state* and not as the antithesis of it. When you learn something new, the neurons in your brain are making connections; this may physically feel like frustration, but it just means your brain is rewiring—literally. Embrace this.

Make It Habitual

Programming is all about learning a bunch of little things that combine to make big things. The best way to learn a lot of little things is through repetition and habit. One way to do this is to simply accept programming as a new part of your lifestyle and do a little bit (or a lot) every day.

Be Creative and Have Personal Projects

It is a good idea to have your own personal programming projects. The more you are personally invested in a project, the more you will learn.

Talk and Teach

One of the best ways to validate your own learning is to teach someone else. If you don't have anyone to teach, then you can substitute this by writing tutorials. This will force you to collect your thoughts and express them clearly.

Keep Going

Our final piece of advice is to simply *stick with it.*

Best of luck!

If you have any questions or comments, you can find us at:
http://www.javascriptforsoundartists.com

William Turner
Steve Leonard

1 Overview and Setup

■ What Is a Program?

A program is any set of instructions that are created or followed. In this book, we focus on writing computer programs, which are lists of instructions that a computer carries out. These instructions can be written and stored in various forms. Some of the first modern computers used punched cards, switches, and cables. Early analogue music synthesizers were a type of computer that used a patchbay style interface to manually allow a programmer to create specific sounds.

■ What Is JavaScript?

JavaScript is a multipurpose programming language initially created to aid developers in adding dynamic features to websites. The language was initially created in 11 days and released in 1995 by a company called Netscape. Developed by Brendan Eich, its original release name was LiveScript. When Netscape introduced support for the language in its browser, LiveScript was renamed JavaScript. Although JavaScript is similar in name to the Java programming language, they are completely unrelated. Today, JavaScript is used in everything from robotics to home automation systems.

DOI: 10.1201/9781003201496-1

◼ HTML, CSS, and JavaScript

The three main technologies used to build websites and web applications are HTML, CSS, and JavaScript.

HTML stands for *hypertext markup language* and is the standard by which we create documents for the World Wide Web. You program HTML by writing elements (sometimes referred to as tags for brevity). These elements contain text and other nested elements, which make up the document's content.

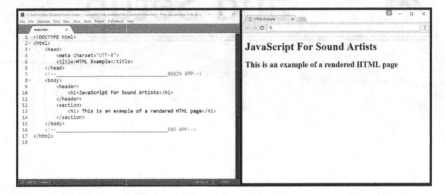

CSS stands for *cascading style sheets* and is a tool used to modify how HTML elements and text are presented. CSS is primarily a visual design tool. For example, with CSS you could modify an HTML element and give it an orange background, change its font size, place it vertically or horizontally, or perform any number of creative visual changes.

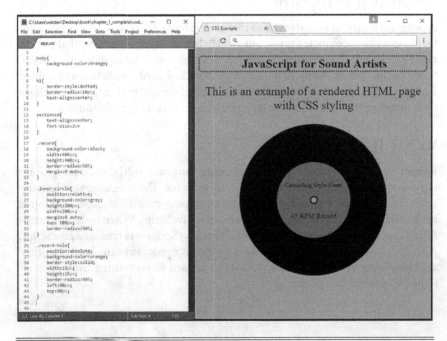

JavaScript is used to add interactive responses to user input. Every time a user clicks, scrolls, taps, moves the mouse cursor, types, or performs an interactive event, JavaScript code can be triggered to change the page in some manner. The JavaScript language was initially designed to perform these functions within the context of designing websites and applications.

▍▊ What Is a Web Application?

A web application is any website that contains more than static, non-interactive pages. This means that, in a web application, the pages have some interactive components in addition to the static text and images displayed. In the early days of the World Wide Web, websites were composed mostly of collections of static documents connected through highlighted text called hyperlinks. These static pages had no interaction with databases. In the early 1990s, this began to change, and web developers began creating websites that had features similar to desktop applications that allowed users to interact with the page via form fields, buttons, and other interactive means to send data over a web server to and from a database.

Early web applications were slow and limited by the technology of the time. In the early 2000s, a culmination of technical shifts that included client-side-rather than server-side-focused web applications helped make web applications more responsive. Part of this shift is attributable to a technology called AJAX (asynchronous JavaScript and XML). This technology pushed dynamic web application development forward by allowing the browser to retrieve and send data to a web server without having to automatically refresh the page in the process. As the J in AJAX indicates, JavaScript is central to this technology, and web applications began to approach the interactive speed of their desktop counterparts.

As you might expect, within the audio world there were attempts to leverage this new technology, which resulted in browser-based audio players, editors, and musical instruments. Many of these applications were initially written using a technology called Flash. This is a proprietary technology that required the user to download and install an additional plug-in to run all programs written in it.

In 2008, a newer version of the HTML standard was written, called HTML-5. This version included an audio player that could directly stream sound files off a web server using a single line of HTML code. The player also included built-in, user-facing controls for play, fast-forward, rewind, pause, stop, loop, and other actions. However, for serious audio development, this was inadequate. Web application developers and audio aficionados wanted something more fully featured.

▍▊ What Is the Web Audio API?

The Web Audio API is a series of exposed code pieces that you can use to accomplish musical and audio tasks in a web browser with less effort than if you were to create them all from scratch. The unexposed portion of the Web Audio API lies in the web browser's source code and is written in whatever language the web browser itself is written in. The technical core of web browsers is usually written in multiple lower-level languages, which can include (but are not limited to) C++, Java, and machine language.

To understand the Web Audio API, you must first understand what an API is. API stands for *application programming interface*. An API is a portion of code that a programmer is given access to, which controls a larger unseen body of code within certain constraints. Imagine if, in order to learn how to play your favorite musical instrument, you had to literally build it from scratch. As you can imagine, this would get very tedious—especially if the instrument were to break. Thus, it's much more convenient to learn to play a premade musical instrument. The convenience here is that the construction process is removed and your only concern is what is important to you, which is the controls needed to use the instrument. In a similar manner, programmers write APIs that expose only small pieces of code for developers to use, and these small pieces of code allow you to do a lot of work with minimal effort.

In addition to being able to load and play back sound files, the Web Audio API also allows you to generate sound from scratch in the form of oscillators. You can then manipulate any sound playback or generation using filters, reverb effects, dynamic compressors, delay effects, and a host of other options.

▌ Setting Up Your Work Environment

To begin working, you must first determine what browser you are going to troubleshoot with. In real-world environments, you would use a test suite to troubleshoot among different browsers and platforms. In this book, we are going to keep things simple and only use the Brave Browser. Brave is built on the same technology as Google Chrome but unlike Chrome, Brave makes user privacy a first class feature. The next thing you need is a code editor. For the exercises, we assume you will be using the Sublime Text editor. Technically, you can use any code editor you want, but Sublime Text is offered as a free trial download and is extremely powerful and widely used. We think it's worth your investment of time to learn it.

The next thing you need to do is create a folder with a basic work template.

1. If you are not already using it, go to this URL to download and install Brave: https://brave.com/.

2. Go to http://www.sublimetext.com/ and download and install Sublime Text.

3. Create a folder on your desktop or in a directory and call it *web audio template*.

4. Open Sublime Text, and in the window that appears, type the following code into it. Then save the file (go to the File menu in Sublime Text and click *Save As*) as *index.html* and choose your *web audio template* folder as the directory to save it in.

```
<!DOCTYPE html>
<html>
    <head>
        <meta charset="UTF-8">
        <title>app</title>
        <script src="js/app.js"></script>
        <link rel="stylesheet" href="css/app.css">
    </head>
    <!--_____BEGIN APP-->
    <body>

    </body>
    <!--_____END APP-->
</html>
```

In your computer's operating system set Brave as the default browser to open HTML documents.

If you are using **Linux** right click the index.html document and go to **properties/open with/** and choose **Brave** and click **Set as Default.**

If you are using **Windows** right click the index.html document and choose **Open with** and select **Brave**.

If you are using **Mac** right click the index.html document and choose **Get Info** and **Open with**. Select **Brave**

Setting Brave as the default browser is done for convenience as it will be useful when running web programs from Sublime text.

5. Inside the web audio template folder, create another folder called css.

6. In Sublime Text, create a new file by going to the File menu and click *New*. Save this file in your css folder as app.css. Leave the contents of this file empty.

7. In the web audio template folder, create another folder called js.

8. Create a new empty document in Sublime Text, then type "use strict" (including quotations and semicolon) at the top of it and save it as app. js in the js folder you just created. This places your JavaScript in strict mode. Strict mode is a restrictive form of JavaScript that enforces better programming practices. All JavaScript code examples in this book will assume you have strict mode enabled.

You are now going to add a few extensions to Sublime Text that will make working with the editor easier in the long term. To do this, you must first download and install the package manager plug-in. Go to the following link and follow the directions on the left side of the window: https://packagecontrol.io/installation. When done, close the console by entering the keys: Ctrl + ` (apostrophe, on the key with the ~).

1. In the Sublime Text menu, go to *Tools>Command Palette*, and in the form field that appears, type install. You should see an option menu appear that says *Package control: Install package*. Click this menu option.

2. Another form field with a series of options appears. This form field allows you to search and explore various plug-ins for Sublime Text. You are now going to install a plug-in that allows you to create a local web server that will be necessary when working with audio files. In the form field, type Sublime server. A list of search results should appear. Click the first one. Look at the bottom of the Sublime Text window, and you should see "installing" in small text. When this process is done, quit and restart Sublime Text. We will cover the specifics of the web server in a later chapter. But rest assured that this setup will be time well spent. To verify that the plug-in is installed, go to *Tools > SublimeServer > Start SublimeServer*. Open your web browser to http://localhost:8080/, and it should display *SublimeServer* at the top of the page.

▮ How to View in Browser

It is useful to know how to open HTML files into your web browser directly from within SublimeText. To do this, drag an html file into SublimeText, right click the contents on the page, and click "Open in Browser". Your web browser will open the selected HTML file.

▮ How to Create Code Snippets

It can be helpful to know how to create code snippets that you can access without writing them out character-by-character every time. Thankfully, Sublime Text has a feature that allows you to do this with snippets. To create a snippet, do the following steps:

1. In Sublime Text menu, go to *Tools > New Snippet*.

2. In the window that appears, delete everything on line 3 and paste the following text: This is a test snippet.

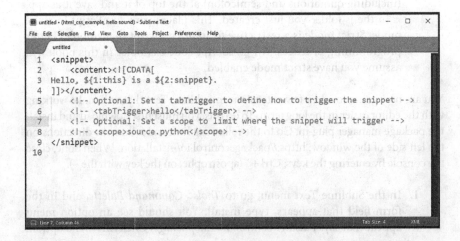

3. On line 6, remove the <!-- and --> characters and type the word test in between the two elements. The result should look like this: *<tabTrigger> test </tabTrigger>*.

```
🖼 untitled • (html_css_example, hello sound) - Sublime Text                              —    □    ✕
File   Edit   Selection   Find   View   Goto   Tools   Project   Preferences   Help

     untitled            ●
 1   <snippet>
 2       <content><![CDATA[
 3   This is a test snippet
 4   ]]></content>
 5       <!-- Optional: Set a tabTrigger to define how to trigger the snippet -->
 6       <tabTrigger>test</tabTrigger>
 7       <!-- Optional: Set a scope to limit where the snippet will trigger -->
 8       <!-- <scope>source.python</scope> -->
 9   </snippet>
10   |

🖵 Line 10, Column 1                                              Tab Size: 4         XML
```

4. Save the file in the default directory that appears and call it *test. sublime-snippet*.

5. Open your *index.html* file in Sublime Text, type the word test, then tap the TAB button on your keyboard. The phrase "this is a test snippet" should appear in the editor.

▮▮ Accessing the Developer Tools

The Brave Browser has a built-in suite of troubleshooting tools called the Developer Tools. You can access these tools by opening the browser and using the key commands:

Windows OS or Linux: Ctrl+Shift+J
Mac: Command+Option+J

We are not going to go over the utility of the developer tools just yet, but they will be highlighted throughout the book.

▮▮ Troubleshooting Problems and Getting Help

If you have any trouble, try using search engines to research solutions. One very good resource is http://stackoverflow.com, which is a community of programmers who ask and answer questions. They have a nice section on JavaScript as well as a lively Web Audio API community that you can find at: http://stackoverflow.com/questions/tagged/web-audio.

2 Getting Started with JavaScript and the Web Audio API

◼ Hello Sound Program

In an introduction to a programming language, the first program you write is often called "Hello World", which prints the words "Hello World" on the screen. Because we are using the Web Audio API to create sounds, this section explains how to create a "Hello Sound" application that immediately plays a sound when you run it.

Copy the folder *web audio template* from the last chapter to a new directory, and rename the copy to *hello_sound*. Open the Sublime text editor and drag the hello_sound folder to it.

Type the code below into the *app.js* file that is present within the *hello_sound* folder and save it.

```
const audioContext = new AudioContext();
let osc = audioContext.createOscillator();
osc.type = "sine";
osc.connect(audioContext.destination);
osc.start(audioContext.currentTime);
```

In Sublime go to **tools/Sublime Server/** and select **Start Sublime Server**. This will start a web server. In your web browser go to http://localhost:8080 and select the folder titled *hello_sound*. You will hear an oscillator.

DOI: 10.1201/9781003201496-2

After you verify that the Hello Sound program works, close the browser. You just wrote your first Web Audio API program!

The code you just ran is a basic oscillator generation and playback script. The first line in the script is called the "Audio Context" and this tells the browser that you are using the Web Audio API. The next line of code creates an oscillator. The third line of code assigns a waveform type to the oscillator, whereas line four connects the oscillator to a virtual audio output called the *destination*, which is analogous to the speakers of your computer. The last line starts the oscillator playing.

If you were to run the previous code on a public web server (as opposed to privately on your local web server), it will not play unless the user enables the web audio API via a gesture such as a mouse click or other action. For this, we will need to write additional code. To see a warning about this problem, refresh the browser and open the developer tools. A warning stating "The AudioContext was not allowed to start. It must be resumed (or created) after a user gesture on the page" is presented.

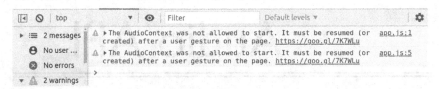

The code to fix the error is presented below. Remove the previous code and replace it with the following code.

```
const audioContext = new AudioContext();
document.addEventListener("mousedown", function() {
    let osc = audioContext.createOscillator();
    osc.type = "sine";
    osc.connect(audioContext.destination);
    osc.start(audioContext.currentTime);

});
```

When you launch the web server and click the webpage an oscillator will play. The code used to trigger the oscillator when the page is clicked is called an event listener. The event listener is the portion of code that looks like this:

```
document.addEventListener("mousedown", function() {

}
```

In the example below, all web audio code *except* the AudioContext is placed inside the event listener.

```
const audioContext = new AudioContext();
document.addEventListener("mousedown", function() {
    let osc = audioContext.createOscillator();
    osc.type = "sine";
```

```
osc.connect(audioContext.destination);
osc.start(audioContext.currentTime);

});
```

A more sophisticated version of the above code is written below. The following code lets you toggle the oscillator on and off when the page is clicked:

```
const audioContext = new AudioContext(); //___Initializes web audio
  api
let osc;
function playOsc(oscType, freq) {
if(osc){
osc.stop(audioContext.currentTime);
console.log("Stopped");
osc = undefined;
}else{
osc = audioContext.createOscillator();
osc.type = oscType;
osc.frequency.value = freq;
osc.connect(audioContext.destination);
osc.start(audioContext.currentTime);
console.log("Start")
}
}
document.addEventListener("mousedown", function() {
    playOsc("sine", 330);
});
```

Don't worry about knowing how the code works just yet; we are going to cover detailed operation of the Web Audio API in future chapters. First, though, we need to cover the basics of the JavaScript language.

▐ Variables

One of the first steps in writing a program is understanding variables and variable assignment. Variables are word forms that are used to store data. For example:

```
let waveformType = "sawtooth";
```

The variable here is named waveformType. This is preceded by the let keyword. The let keyword is a variable declaration keyword. You always specify the variable declaration keyword prior to declaring the variable. *Declaring* a variable means you are *creating a new variable*. JavaScript has three different variable declaration keywords and they are **const, let**, and **var**. In this chapter, we go over the let and const declaration and in later chapters you learn about var. After typing the declaration keyword you type a space and give a name to your variable. Variable names are typically a reflection of the thing they represent. In this case, the variable is being used to describe a type of oscillator waveform, so is named waveformType. You probably noticed the odd capitalization of the word "type" in waveformType. The convention of capitalizing words to distinguish them within variable names is called *camel case*. This convention is used because variable names cannot contain white space to separate them. If you rewrote the variable in the following manner, you get an error:

```
let waveform type = "sawtooth"; //____returns an error
```

Type the above code into the app.js file of your *hello_sound* template. Launch the browser and open the developer tools by right clicking on the page and selecting "inspect" or using the key command (**Windows:** Ctrl+Shift+I or **Mac:** Command+Option+I). Inside the console tab you should see an error similar to the one in the following image.

The text in red is the actual error and is identified as a syntax error. Directly to the right of the error you can see the file and the line number where the error occurred. This number corresponds to the line number in your file, which might differ from the one in the image. After you see the error, remove the line you added that is causing the error in app.js and save the file.

After you declare and name a variable, you can assign some data to it. You use the assignment operator "=" to do this.

It is important to understand that in JavaScript the "=" symbol is not called the "equal sign" and its functionality *does not* mean *equal to*. The "=" symbol indicates assignment, so it is called the assignment operator. The value on the right side of the assignment operator contains the data you want to assign to the variable name on the left side. In the following example, the string "sawtooth" is assigned to the variable waveformType:

```
let waveformType = "sawtooth";
```

When you assign a string of words to a variable, you must place them between quotation marks. The resulting data type is called a string. Data types represent the types of data that you can use in your program. Different programming languages have different data types. JavaScript has eight data types and one of these is the *string* data type (see Chapter 6 for a list of JavaScript data types).

After you assign data to your variable, you must end the variable declaration with a semicolon.

In summary, there are five parts to a variable declaration:

- The   declaration   keyword

- The   variable name

- The   assignment operator

- The   data you wish to assign to the variable

- The   closing semi colon

You can assign multiple variables at once using the following syntax:

```
let osc1 = 1200,
osc2 = 1300,
osc3 = 100;
```

When using the let keyword to declare variables you can *reassign* them as in this example.

```
let osc = 500;
console.log(osc) // 500
osc = 1000;
console.log(osc) // 1000
```

Declaring variables with let more than once in the same scope will create an error. You will learn more about *scope* in later chapters.

```
let osc = 500;
let osc = 1000; // error, variable already declared.
```

The const declaration behaves differently than let. Const is used with variables that the developer intends to remain unchanged after being declared. If you declare a variable with const and assign it a primitive data type such as a number or string you will get an error if you change it.

```
const osc = 1000;
osc = 1000 // reassignment gives an error
```

In some cases, you might want to declare a variable and not assign data to it, as in the following example:

```
let waveformType;
```

If you do this using let, JavaScript automatically assigns undefined to it. You can also assign undefined explicitly like this:

```
let waveformType = undefined;
```

The keyword **undefined** is another JavaScript data type. Notice that **undefined** is not enclosed in quotation marks because it is not a string but represents a data type.

If you declare a variable using **const** and do not explicitly assign a value to it, the interpreter will return an error.

```
const osc; // SyntaxError: Missing initializer in const declaration
```

Null

The primitive value null is similar to the primitive value undefined. Both can act as a placeholder for empty variables. When the type of operator (discussed later in this chapter) is used to determine the type of null, the result is object. This is not what you might expect and is a flaw in the language. The correct returned value should be null. Because of this, I suggest you never use null and always use undefined.

Documenting Your Code with Comments

When you are programming, it is a good habit to type messages into your code that are intended to be read by human beings (yourself or others) and not be interpreted by the computer. These messages are called *comments*. You can write either single or multi-line comments into your program and they look like this.

```
// This is a single line comment.
//It begins with two forward slash characters
//These end at the end of the line
/* This is a multi-line comment and begins with a forward slash and
   asterisk. It ends with an asterisk and a forward slash */
```

In a real-world scenario, we might comment on our code like this:

```
let waveformType = "sawtooth"; // oscillator value
```

All the characters from the // to the end of the line are ignored by the computer.

Exploring Variables with an Oscillator

Now that you understand what variables are, the following example shows how you use them:

Open up the code you wrote at the beginning of this chapter and add the variable waveformType to it, as in the following code:

```
const audioContext = new AudioContext();
let waveformType = "sawtooth"; //___added variable
let osc = audioContext.createOscillator();
osc.type = "sine";
osc.connect(audioContext.destination);
osc.start(audioContext.currentTime);
```

Replace the osc.type assignment with the waveformType variable like this:

```
const audioContext = new AudioContext();
let waveformType = "sawtooth"; //___added variable
let osc = audioContext.createOscillator();
osc.type = waveformType; //__Assigned it to our oscillator type
osc.connect(audioContext.destination);
osc.start(audioContext.currentTime);
```

Launch your web browser, and instead of hearing a sine waveform, you should hear a sawtooth waveform.

In this example, the following declarations assign values to variables that represent other waveform types.

```
const audioContext = new AudioContext();
//___ 4 variables that represent oscillator waveforms
let saw = "sawtooth";
let sine = "sine";
let tri = "triangle";
let square = "square";
//___ A variable intended to contain one of these waveforms
let currentWaveform = undefined;
currentWaveform = square;
//_____Start of oscillator
let osc = audioContext.createOscillator();
osc.type = currentWaveform; // Assigned it to our oscillator type
osc.connect(audioContext.destination);
osc.start(audioContext.currentTime);
```

Each of the four new variables contains a string that represents an oscillator waveform type. The square variable is assigned to the currentWaveform variable in the following line:

```
currentWaveform = square;
```

Notice that no new declaration is required for the currentWaveform variable to assign (and replace) whatever was previously assigned to it. The new data on the right side of "=" is assigned to currentWaveform. If you launch your web browser you will hear a square wave play. In programming being able to overwrite variables in this manner is referred to as mutability (changeability), and we say that variables are mutable. The opposite of this is called immutability.

▌ console.log()

When programs begin to get big, it can be difficult to know what value is assigned to a variable at any given moment. One way you can find out is by using a built-in feature called console.log().

The way you do this is by typing console.log() into your code at the point where you want to check a given variables assignment. You then place the *variable name* inside the parenthesis. You can also add a message to console.log() by placing a comma after the variable and writing a message in quotes.

To see what the currentWaveform variable has as its assignment, you do this:

```
const audioContext = new AudioContext();
//_____Added 4 variables that represent oscillator
   waveforms
let saw = "sawtooth";
let sine = "sine";
let tri = "triangle";
let square = "square";
```

```
let currentWaveform = undefined;
currentWaveform = square;
console.log(currentWaveform, "The waveform type"); //___ square
//_____Start of oscillator
let osc = audioContext.createOscillator();
osc.type = currentWaveform; // Assigned it to our oscillator type
osc.connect(audioContext.destination);
osc.start(audioContext.currentTime);
```

If you launch Brave, open the developer tools and click the console tab, you will see the output of our console.log().

One thing to remember is that because variables can have different values at different times, the output of console.log() depends on where it is placed in the program. If you modify the last example and place console.log() immediately after the currentWaveform variable which has undefined assigned to it, then undefined is output to the log.

```
//_____A variable intended to contain one of these waveforms
let currentWaveform = undefined;
console.log(currentWaveform); //_____results in "undefined"
currentWaveform = square;
```

So far we've mentioned three of the seven data types in JavaScript. The first was string, the second was undefined, and the last was null.

Before we go further let's explore the string data type a bit more in depth.

▌ String

As we already discovered, strings are denoted by quotation marks. The variable below is a string:

```
let oscillator = "square";
```

You can manipulate strings in different ways. One of the most common is by combining multiple strings into one string. This is called concatenation and it works by using the plus sign (+) like this:

```
let oscillator = "saw" + "tooth";
console.log(oscillator); // sawtooth
```

Here is another example of concatenating two variables and storing them in a new variable.

```
let phrase = "This sound is an ";
let soundType = "oscillator";
let sentence = phrase + soundType;
console.log(sentence); // "This sound is an oscillator".
```

Another way to combine strings is with string interpolation using template literals. A template literal uses the "${}" syntax. For template literals, back ticks are used to create a string and variables are placed in the curly braces after a dollar sign.

```
let phrase = "This sound is an ";
let soundType = "oscillator";
let sentence = `${phrase}${soundType}. Ocillators sound cool!`;
console.log(sentence); // "This sound is an oscillator.Ocillators
  sound cool!".
```

Notice that strings can contain white space.

This is a perfectly valid string even though it contains a lot of white-space characters:

```
let myFavoriteSynthCompany = "My favorite synth company is Moog";
```

If you want to get the number of characters in a string, you can use what is called the *length property* like this:

```
console.log(myFavoriteSynthCompany.length); // 33
```

The output of the length property includes the white-space characters of the string.

▌ Built in String Methods

JavaScript has a series of built-in tools called methods that allow you to manipulate data. Some of these methods are specifically designed to manipulate *string* data.

These are called *string methods.*

To see how to use a string method, take a look at the examples of the toUpperCase() and toLowerCase() methods.

toUpperCase()

This method changes all the characters in a string to uppercase.

```
let oscillator = "sawtooth";
oscillator.toUpperCase(); // SAWTOOTH
```

toLowerCase()

This method changes all the characters in a string to lowercase.

```
let oscillator = "SAWTOOTH";
oscillator.toLowerCase(); // "sawtooth"
```

Some useful string methods are:

charAt()	Returns a character at any given index in a string
replace()	Finds and replaces a group of characters in a string
slice()	Extracts part of a string

You do not need to immediately memorize how each of these string methods works, but it is a good idea to know about them. This way, when you do need to implement any of the functionality they provide, you know which tool to reach for. If you would like to explore more string methods, a good resource is the Mozilla Developer network at: https://developer.mozilla.org/en-US/docs/Web/JavaScript/Reference/Global_Objects/String.

Let's go through each one of these and explain how to use them.

charAt()

This method gets a character at any given index value within a string. For example, if you have the string "oscillator-1" and want to know what the second letter of this string is without actually looking at it, you can do this:

```
let sound = "oscillator";
console.log(sound.charAt(1)); // "s"
```

Now you might be wondering why charAt(1) would give us back "s" and not "o". The reason is that the count begins at zero. So if we wanted the first letter we would do this:

```
console.log(sound.charAt(0)); // "o"
```

When an index list begins with zero it is called a *zero-based index*.

replace()

This method finds a group of characters in a string and replaces them with another string. If you want to replace an entire word you can do it like this:

```
let myFavoriteSynthCompany = "My favorite synth company is Moog.
  Moog is great!";
let myNewFavoriteSynthCompany = myFavoriteSynthCompany.
  replace("Moog","Dave Smith Instruments");
console.log(myNewFavoriteSynthCompany); // My favorite synth
  company is Dave Smith Instruments. Moog is great!
```

As you probably noticed, when using the replace method in this manner it only replaces the first instance of the word you select. To replace all instances of the word, you need to use the following syntax to *globally* replace them in the string.

```
let myFavoriteSynthCompany = "My favorite synth company is Moog.
  Moog is great!";
let myNewFavoriteSynthCompany = myFavoriteSynthCompany.replace(/
  Moog/gi,"Dave Smith Instruments");
console.log(myNewFavoriteSynthCompany); // My favorite synth company
  is Dave Smith Instruments. Dave Smith Instruments is great!
```

The g stands for global and the i denotes case *insensitivity*. If you wanted the string replacement to be case-sensitive you would simply use a g and omit the i. These characters are part of a pattern matching language for string data called regular expressions. Regular expressions are an advanced topic that will not be covered further in this book.

slice()

This method extracts part of a string.

```
let oscillator = "sawtooth";
let sound = oscillator.slice(0,3);
console.log(sound); // saw
```

Like charAt(), slice() works on a zero-based index. This means the first character is always 0. The slice method takes two values: a beginning index value and an ending index value. When a method takes values they are called *arguments*. The charAt() method takes one argument. The slice() method takes two arguments. The slice method's first argument is where the slice starts, and this value is included in the slice. The second value is where the slice ends and is non-inclusive. This means all the characters up to but not including the second value are included in the slice.

▌ The Length Property

The length property is an additional tool that allows you to get the number of characters in a string. A *property* looks similar to a method but does not include parenthesis and does not require arguments to return a value. The character count of the length property starts at one and *not* zero.

```
let instrument = "piano";
console.log(instrument.length); // 5
```

If you want to get the last value of a string, you can combine the length property with the charAt() method. This allows you to retrieve the last character in a string in a manner that doesn't require you to know how long the string is. The code shows an example of this. The reason you subtract 1 from the length property is because the length property begins counting at one while charAt() begins counting at zero. Therefore, you subtract one from the length property to compensate for the offset.

```
let sound = "oscillator-1";
let oscNumber = sound.charAt(sound.length - 1);
console.log(oscNumber); // 1
```

▌ Numbers

In JavaScript, numbers are a distinct data type. Below is a variable named frequencyValue and it is assigned a number of 200. It is then assigned to the oscillators pitch. If you place the code below in a new JavaScript file and run it, you will hear an oscillator play at a frequency of 200 Hz. Modify the number value assigned to the frequencyValue variable and launch the code to hear the oscillator play at different pitches.

```
const audioContext = new AudioContext();
let frequencyValue = 200; //___Create variable frequencyValue
let waveform = "sawtooth";
```

```
let osc = audioContext.createOscillator();
osc.type = waveform;
//_____ assign it to the oscillators pitch
osc.frequency.value = frequencyValue;
osc.connect(audioContext.destination);
osc.start(audioContext.currentTime);
```

■ How to Determine the Data Type of a Variable?

You can discern the difference between data types in variables by using the typeof operator.

```
let waveform = "sine";
let polyphony = 16;
console.log(typeof waveform); // string
console.log(typeof polyphony); // number
```

Unlike strings, numbers do not use quotation marks. In fact, if you did use a number with quotation marks its data type would *not* be number, it would be *string*.

Here's an example:

```
let oscillators = " 6 ";
let polyphony = 6;
console.log(typeof oscillators); // string
console.log(typeof polyphony); // number
```

You can do basic math with numbers using the following symbols. These symbols are called arithmetic operators.

+	Addition
−	Subtraction
*	Multiplication
/	Division
%	Modulo

Examples of Arithmetic Operators

```
console.log(5 + 5); // 10
console.log(10 − 5); // 5
console.log(5 * 5); // 25
console.log(25 / 5); // 5
console.log(10 % 9); // 1
```

The last symbol (%) might be new to you and it's pronounced **moj**-*uh*-loh. The purpose of this symbol is to output the remainder of a division. So for example:

```
console.log(12 % 9); // This would equal 3
```

The precedent rules of algebra also apply. If you wrap a calculation in parenthesis, the calculation inside the parenthesis is performed first.

Example

```
let oscillator1 = 1000;
let oscillator2 = 100;
let oscillator3 = 20;
let combinedOscillator = oscillator1 +(oscillator2 * oscillator3);
console.log( combinedOscillator); // 3000
```

If you want to do more elaborate calculations, JavaScript has a built-in tool called the Math object which allows you to use a collection of math methods to manipulate numbers.

So, for example, if we wanted to round a decimal number to its nearest integer, you can use

Math.round() like this:

```
Math.round(1000.789) // outputs 1001
```

Some useful math object methods are:

Math.min()	Finds the smallest number in a collection of numbers
Math.max()	Finds the largest number in a collection of numbers
Math.ceil()	Rounds a decimal number up to the nearest integer and removes the decimal values
Math.floor()	Removes the decimal values of a number, making it an integer
Math.random()	Creates a random number between 0 and 1
Math.abs()	Returns the absolute value of a number

Let's go over each of these one by one. If you would like to explore more math methods, a good site is the Mozilla Developer Network at: https://developer.mozilla.org/en-US/docs/Web/JavaScript/Reference/Global_Objects/Math.

Math.min() and Math.max()

Math.min() finds the smallest number in a collection of numbers, while Math.max() allows you to find the largest number in a collection of numbers.

```
Math.min(5000, 2000, 80); // 80
Math.max(5000, 2000, 80); // 5000
//_____With variables
let freq_1 = 5000;
let freq_2 = 2000;
let freq_3 = 80;
Math.min(freq_1, freq_2, freq_3); // 80
Math.max(freq_1, freq_2, freq_3); // 5000
```

Math.ceil() and Math.floor()

These two methods turn a decimal number into an integer. Math.ceil() rounds up to the next higher integer value if there are any non-zero digits to the right of the

---

decimal, while Math.floor() keeps the integer value after discarding the digits to the right of the decimal.

```
Math.ceil(3.00333); // 4
Math.floor(3.9999); // 3
```

Math.random()

The random method creates a random number between zero and one.

```
let randomNumber = Math.random();
console.log(randomNumber); // example: 0.019790495047345757
```

You can combine Math.random() with Math.floor() to create a random number between two values. The expression in the following example creates a random integer between 20 and 20,000.

```
let max = 20000;
let min = 20;
let randomInteger = Math.floor(Math.random() * (max - min + 1) +
  min);
console.log(randomInteger); // Between 20 and 20000
```

Math.abs()

The abs method allows you to get the absolute value of a number.

```
let num = Math.abs(-100);
console.log(num); // 100
```

This is useful for finding the difference between numeric variables of unknown values.

```
let a = 1000;
let b = 5000;
console.log(Math.abs(b - a)); // 4000
```

▮ Number to String Conversion

If you want to convert between numbers and numeric strings, you can use the following techniques.

To convert a string to a number, place the plus symbol (+) before the string like this:

```
let numericString = "120";
let num = +numericString; // plus symbol
console.log(num); // 120
console.log(typeof num); // number
```

If you want to convert a number to a numeric string, concatenate the number with an empty string like this:

```
let num = 80;
let numericString = num + "";
console.log( numericString ); // 80
console.log(typeof numericString); // string
```

If you attempt to do a math operation using non-numeric values, sometimes you will receive a returned value of NaN. This stands for not a number. Here is an example of attempting to add two values in which one value is a number and the other is not.

```
let osc1 = undefined;
let osc2 = 200;
console.log( osc1 + osc2 ); // NaN
```

■ BigInt

As of this writing, the newest JavaScript data type is BigInt. BigInt lets you work with integers that are larger than what is allowed using the number data type. To demonstrate the problem it solves, look at the following code:

```
console.log(9999999999999999); // 10000000000000000
```

The behavior above is called integer overflow and it happens when you attempt to create a number that exceeds what JavaScript can represent by a given number of digits. If you need to work with very large integers, you can use BigInt to represent them. The syntax to convert a number to a BigInt requires that you append the letter "n" to the number that you want to convert.

```
let someLargeInteger = 9999999999999999n;
// to inspect the value you need to use the toValue() method
console.log(someLargeInteger.valueOf()) // 9999999999999999n
```

Basic arithmetic operators work on BigInt and Math methods do not. Working with BigInts is an advanced topic and when working with numbers we will be using the number data type for the rest of the book.

■ Arrays

Arrays are a construct that holds multiple pieces of data. You can think of them as variables that hold more than one item. Arrays are expressed using brackets, where each item is separated by a comma. Each item in the array is designated an index number with the first item starting at zero.

```
let waveforms = [ ]; // empty array
let waveforms = ["square","sawtooth","triangle","sine"]; // array
  with some data
```

If you want to access any of this data, you can use the following notation:

```
waveforms[0]; // square
waveforms[1]; // sawtooth
```

```
waveforms[2]; // triangle
waveforms[3]; // sine
waveforms[4]; // undefined ( no data )
```

If you want to know how many items are inside an array, use the length property like this:

```
let waveforms = ["square", "sawtooth", "triangle", "sine"];
waveforms.length; // 4
```

Arrays come with built-in methods that you can use to manipulate the data in them. A full list of these is available at the Mozilla developer network at this URL: https://developer.mozilla.org/en-US/docs/Web/JavaScript/Reference/Global_Objects/Array. We are only going to go over a handful of these and they are:

push()	Adds additional items to the end of an array
pop()	Removes a single item from the end of an array
shift()	Removes a single item from the beginning of an array
unshift()	Adds additional items to the beginning of an array
concat()	Concatenates arrays together into one array

push()

This method adds items to the end of an array.

```
let synthFrequencies = [5000, 1000, 500];
synthFrequencies.push(100); // This places a new item at the end of
  the array
console.log (synthFrequencies); // [5000,1000,500,100]
```

You can use the push method to add multiple items at once.

```
let synthFrequencies = [5000, 1000, 500];
synthFrequencies.push(100, 50, 30);
console.log(synthFrequencies); // [ 5000, 1000, 500, 100, 50, 30]
```

pop()

This method removes a single item at the end of an array.

```
let synthFrequencies = [5000, 1000, 500];
synthFrequencies.pop();
console.log(synthFrequencies); // [ 5000, 1000]
```

If you want to capture the last item you removed from an array in a variable, do this:

```
let synthFrequencies = [5000, 1000, 500];
let lastItem = synthFrequencies.pop();
console.log(lastItem); // 500
```

shift()

This method removes an item from the beginning of an array.

```
let synthFrequencies = [5000, 1000, 500];
synthFrequencies.shift();
console.log(synthFrequencies) // [1000, 500];
```

If you want to capture the first item you removed from an array in a variable, do this:

```
let synthFrequencies = [5000, 1000, 500];
let firstItem = synthFrequencies.shift();
console.log(firstItem); // 5000
```

unshift()

This method adds new items to the beginning of an array.

```
let synthFrequencies = [5000, 1000, 500];
synthFrequencies.unshift(7500, 6000);
console.log(synthFrequencies); // [ 7500, 6000, 5000, 1000, 500 ];
```

concat()

This method merges multiple arrays together into one array.

```
let drumMachines = ["MPC", "Maschine", "TR 808"];
let keyboards = ["Juno", "ARP", "Jupiter"];
let percussion = ["vibraphone", "bongos"];
let stringed = ["guitar", "bass", "harp"]
let instruments = drumMachines.concat(keyboards, percussion,
  stringed);
console.log(instruments); /* [ 'MPC','Maschine','TR 808','Juno','AR
  P','Jupiter','vibraphone', 'bongos','guitar','bass','harp' ] */
```

A tool that you use to copy the content of an array into another array is the destructuring assignment syntax. The syntax consists of three dots and is used like this:

```
let drumMachines = ["MPC", "Maschine", "TR 808"];
let instruments = [...drumMachines,
"Juno", "ARP", "Jupiter",
"vibraphone", "bongos",
"guitar", "bass", "harp"
]
console.log(instruments) /* [ 'MPC','Maschine','TR 808','Juno','ARP
  ','Jupiter','vibraphone', 'bongos','guitar','bass','harp' ] */
```

▌ Summary

In this chapter, you learned about variables, comments, numbers, strings, and arrays. In the next chapter, you will learn about various assignments and logical operators.

3   Operators

You learned about the basic assignment operator (=) and some of the arithmetic operators in the previous chapter. In this chapter, we are going to explore other assignment operators, as well as comparison operators, that allow you to determine the relationship between variables and values, such as whether they have the same value. We will also explore the Boolean data type, which has either a true or a false value that can be assigned to variables or is the result of a comparison operation.

▮ What Are Operators?

Operators represent actions that you use to change the value of a variable, or compare values or variables. The word *operand* is used to describe a value being used in an operation involving operators. So in the following example, the operands are 300 and 400. The output of the comparison is said to be what the expression evaluates to. In the following example, the operation evaluates to false:

```
300 == 400 // The values here (300 and 400) are called operands,
    and the output evaluates to false.
```

Operators fall into arithmetic, assignment, or logical categories. The arithmetic operators that we covered in the previous chapter are used with numbers. The

DOI: 10.1201/9781003201496-3

assignment operators are used to assign values to variables. The logical operators are used to compare two values and return a true or false value based on the result of the comparison.

▌ Assignment Operators

Assignment operators are used to assign data to variables. Here is a list of assignment operators:

Assignment Operator	Name
=	Assignment
+=	Addition assignment
–=	Subtraction assignment
*=	Multiplication assignment
/=	Division assignment
%=	Modulo assignment

▌ Assignment

This operator assigns a value to a variable.

```
let osc = 100;
```

With assignment operators, you can also assign variables to other variables.

```
let osc1 = 100;
let osc2 = osc1;
console.log(osc2); // 100
```

▌ Addition Assignment

This operator increments a numeric variable or appends a string to a variable. In the following example, an oscillator is assigned a value of 100 and then incremented by 100 to give it a value of 200.

```
let osc = 100;
osc += 100;
console.log(osc); // 200
```

To demonstrate the use of the addition assignment operator, the following code sets an ever-increasing frequency change to an oscillator and you can listen to the effect. A method called setInterval() is defined, although the specifics of setInterval() are not important at this time. What *is* important is understanding that the addition assignment operator is incrementing the frequency value by 100 every 0.5 seconds when setInterval() is called.

```
let audioContext = new AudioContext();
let osc = audioContext.createOscillator();
osc.frequency.value = 300;
```

```
osc.connect(audioContext.destination);
osc.start(audioContext.currentTime);
setInterval(function(){
osc.frequency.value += 100; //____Increment frequency value by 100
  every 0.5 seconds
console.log(osc.frequency.value);//____View change
},500);//_____500 milliseconds is 0.5 seconds
```

When you use the addition assignment operator with a string, the string you supply is concatenated with the variable. Here is an example:

```
let keyboards = "";
keyboards += "Korg ";
keyboards += "Yamaha ";
keyboards += "Kurzweil ";
console.log(keyboards); // Korg Yamaha Kurzweil
```

▌ Subtraction Assignment

This operator is used to decrement a numeric variable.

```
let osc = 500;
osc -= 100;
console.log(osc); // 400
```

▌ Multiplication Assignment

This operator multiplies a variable with a value and assigns it to the variable.

```
let osc = 200;
osc *= 2;
osc *= 2;
console.log(osc); // 800
```

▌ Division Assignment

This operator divides a variable by a value and assigns it to the variable.

```
let osc = 200;
osc /= 2;
osc /= 2;
console.log(osc); // 50
```

▌ Modulo Assignment

This operator divides a variable by a value and assigns the *remainder* of that division to the variable.

```
let osc = 200;
osc %= 150;
console.log(osc); // 50
```

▋ The Boolean Data Type

The Boolean data type is either true or false. This is conveyed by the word-form values true and false. Booleans are important because you can use them to program on or off (true or false) values into the code. So, for example, you could use them as a value that toggles an oscillator on or off. Assigning a Boolean value to a variable in JavaScript looks like this:

```
let oscillatorIsOn = true; // true
oscillatorIsOn = false; // changed to false
```

Boolean values can also be the result of the comparison operators described below or used in conditionals statements, which we will cover in the next chapter.

▋ Comparison Operators

Comparison operators are used to compare two variables or values. They output a true or false value depending on whether the variables or values are similar or different from one another in some way. The similarity or difference being tested for is dependent on the operator used. So, for example, if you test whether two values are the same using the strict equality operator (===) and they are not the same, the resulting value is false. There are eight comparison operators.

Comparison Operator	Name
==	Equality operator
===	Strict equality operator
>	Greater than
<	Less than
>=	Greater than or equal to
<=	Less than or equal to
!=	Not equal to
!==	Strict not equal to

▋ Equality Operator

This operator checks whether the left operand is equal to the right operand. It then returns a Boolean value to represent the outcome of the comparison.

```
200 == 200; // true
"200hz" == "200hz"; // true
let osc1 = "200hz";
let osc2 = "200hz";
console.log(osc1 == osc2); // true
```

The equality operator can be a bit tricky because it attempts to do a data type coercion before comparing operands. Data type coercion occurs when the code interpreter (in our case the web browser) attempts to convert one data type into another. In the following example, we compare a number and a numeric string.

JavaScript tries to convert the string to a number before doing the comparison. If the string is a numeric string, the conversion is successful, and the comparison is performed. In this case, the result of the comparison is the Boolean value true because the numeric string "200" is successfully converted to the value 200, which matches the value of osc1.

```
let osc1 = 200;
let osc2 = "200";
console.log(osc1 == osc2); // true
200 == "oscillator" // false
```

▊ Strict Equality Operator

To protect against the confusion of type coercion using the equality operator, you can use the strict equality operator. This operator does *not* do data type coercion. This means that, if *any* numeric string is compared against a number, the result is always false. For newer JavaScript programmers, we suggest that you always use this operator. Restricting yourself to this operator helps to mitigate problems involving coercion before they start.

```
//_____Examples
900 === 900 // true
let osc1 = 200;
let osc2 = "200";
console.log(osc1 === osc2); // false
```

▊ Greater Than and Less Than Operators

These operators produce a Boolean result that is based on whether the left operand is less than or greater than the right operand.

```
100 < 200 // true
300 < 200 // false
300 > 200 // true
300 > 500 // false
```

The greater than and less than operators do data type coercion as shown in this example:

```
600 > "500" // true
600 < "500" // false
```

▊ Greater Than or Equal To Operator

This operator returns a Boolean value of true if the first operand is greater than or equal to the second operand.

```
let osc1 = 300;
let osc2 = 500;
let osc3 = 300;
osc3 >= osc1 // true
osc2 >= osc1 // true
osc1 >= osc2 // false
```

The greater than or equal to operator does data type coercion as shown in this example:

```
300 >= "300" // true
```

▌▌ Less Than or Equal To Operator

This operator returns a Boolean value of true if the left operand is less than or equal to the right operand.

```
300 <= 300 // true
300 <= 500 // true
300 <= 200 // false
```

The less than or equal to operator does data type coercion as shown in these examples:

```
300 <= "300" // true
300 <= "500" // true
300 <= "200" // false
```

▌▌ Not Equal To Operator

This operator is a combination of the NOT symbol and the equal sign. The NOT symbol is expressed as an exclamation mark and is sometimes referred to as the *bang* operator. When NOT is coupled with an equal sign to produce the not equal to operator, it can be used to return a Boolean value that is based on whether two values are not equal to each other. If the two values are *not equal*, the result is true. If the two values are *equal*, the result is false.

```
300 != 200 // true
300 != 300 // false
```

The not equal to operator does data type coercion as shown in this example:

```
"300" != 300 // false
```

▌▌ Strict Not Equal To Operator

This operator returns a Boolean value that is based on whether two values are not equal to each other. The strict not equal to operator, unlike the not equal to operator, does not do type coercion.

```
"300" !== 300 // true
300 !== 300 // false
```

▌▌ Logical Operators

Logical operators allow you to check if a collection of statements is true or false and return a Boolean value based on this information.

Logical Operator	Name
&&	AND
||	OR
!	NOT

▐ The Logical AND Operator

The logical AND operator evaluates to true only if all the operands are true. The way it works is that first, the value on the right side of the operator is evaluated, and if its value is false, the Boolean value of false is returned. In this case, the value on the left side of the operator is never considered!

If the value on the right side of the operator evaluates to true, then and only then does the AND operator check the value on the left side of the operator. If the value on the left side of the operator is false, then the Boolean value false is returned. In the case where both the values on the left and right sides of the logical AND operator are true, the Boolean value true is returned.

```
true && true // true
true && false // false
false && true // false
false && false // false
```

▐ The Logical OR Operator

This operator returns true as long as either of the operands is true.

```
true || true // true
true || false // true
false || true // true
false || false // false
```

▐ The NOT Operator

This operator inverts a Boolean value.

```
!false // true
!true // false
```

Another way to look at this code is that if a value is not false, then it is true, and if its value is not true, then it is false.

In JavaScript, there are six values that evaluate to false. They are the following:

false
""
null
undefined
0
NaN

All other values evaluate to true.

When you specify the NOT operator twice in a row before a variable or an operand, the resultant value is its original Boolean value.

```
!!false // false
!!true // true
!!0 // false
!!"" // false
!!null // false
!!undefined // false
!!NaN // false
```

■ Summary

In this chapter, you learned about JavaScript assignment and logical operators, the Boolean data type, and what values evaluate to false. In the next chapter, you will learn to leverage these tools using two new concepts: conditionals and loops.

4 Conditional Statements, Loops, and Scope

Conditional statements and loops are two of the most widely used constructs in programming. Conditional statements allow your program to make choices based on a set of criteria. Loops use repetition allowing your program to complete many tasks quickly. Scope determines the availability of variables to different parts of your code.

▮ Conditional Statements

To create programs that do more than basic calculations or print text, they must be able to make decisions. You can program these decisions by using *conditional statements*. Conditional statements check if a value is true or false and then execute a branch of code based on this condition. We are going to go over the following three conditional statements:

- if

- switch

- ternary

DOI: 10.1201/9781003201496-4

▌ The If Statement

The syntax of an `if` statement consists of the `if` keyword, a pair of parenthesis, and two curly braces. This is what an empty `if` statement looks like:

```
if(){
}
```

To use an `if` statement, you place a value or condition inside the parenthesis and some code to execute inside the curly braces. If the condition inside the parenthesis evaluates to true, the code inside the curly braces is executed. If the condition evaluates to false, no action is taken and the code inside the curly braces is skipped. In the following code, an `if` statement is used to check if an oscillator frequency is set to 80 Hz prior to play start. If it is, the oscillator plays; if it is not, the code inside the curly braces is ignored and the oscillator does not play.

```
//_____BEGIN Setup
const audioContext = new AudioContext();
let osc = audioContext.createOscillator();
osc.type = "sawtooth";
osc.frequency.value = 80;
osc.connect(audioContext.destination);
//_____END Setup
//_____BEGIN Check frequency
if(osc.frequency.value === 80){
osc.start(audioContext.currentTime);
}
//_____END Check frequency
```

If statements can also have an optional `else` branch that executes if the initial condition evaluates to false. In the following code, the `if` statement checks to see if `frequency.value` is 100 Hz. If this condition is true, the oscillator begins playing. If this condition is false, the `else` branch executes, assigns `frequency.value` to 50 Hz, and starts the oscillator playing.

```
//_____BEGIN Setup
const audioContext = new AudioContext();
let osc = audioContext.createOscillator();
osc.type = "sawtooth";
osc.frequency.value = 200;
osc.connect(audioContext.destination);
//_____END Setup
//_____BEGIN Conditional
if(osc.frequency.value === 100){
//__evaluates to false
osc.start(audioContext.currentTime);
}else{
//__So this plays
osc.frequency.value = 50;
osc.start(audioContext.currentTime);
```

```
}
//_____END Conditional
```

Suppose you want to check for more than two conditions and do something different for each one. You can do this by creating an `if` statement with multiple `else if` branches in sequence. The final `else` statement catches all conditions that were not met along the way. An empty example looks like this:

```
if(){
}
else if(){
}
else{
}
```

In the following working example, the code executes and checks to see if `osc.type` is set to "`sine`". If this condition evaluates to false, the else if branch runs and checks if the oscillator type is set to "`sawtooth`". This evaluates to true and the oscillator starts playing. If osc.type is not set to "`sine`" or "`sawtooth`" (in other words, if both conditions are evaluated to false), then the result is the execution of `console.log()`, which outputs "no condition met".

```
let audioContext = new AudioContext();
let osc = audioContext.createOscillator();
osc.type = "sawtooth";
osc.connect(audioContext.destination);
if(osc.type === "sine"){
osc.start(audioContext.currentTime);
}else if(osc.type === "sawtooth"){
osc.frequency.value = 50;
osc.start(audioContext.currentTime);
}else{
console.log("no condition met");
}
```

▌ The Switch Statement

If you catch yourself writing an `if` statement with a lot of `else if` branches, you should consider using a `switch` statement. A `switch` statement allows you to check if a variable has a particular value assigned to it and then runs a block of code that begins where that value is defined. The following code is an example of an empty `switch` statement. The expression in parenthesis determines a value. The `case` statements define values that you want to catch and then run some code. Each case statement is terminated by a `break` statement because otherwise the code following the `break` statement is run. At the end of the `switch` statement, you can define the optional `default` keyword that specifies the code to run if none of the other `case` statements evaluate to true (the value is not one that you expected).

```
switch(expression){
case "value1": //__if true
//_____then do something
break;
```

```
  case "value2": //__if true
//_____then do something
break;
default: //____if all other cases are false
//_____then do this
}
```

The following code is an example of a `switch` statement that checks the value of an oscillator type and sets its frequency value based on its being a sine, sawtooth, or square wave. If the oscillator is not one of these types, the default branch executes and sets `osc.frequency.value` to 200.

```
//_____BEGIN Setup
let audioContext = new AudioContext();
let osc = audioContext.createOscillator();
osc.type = "sawtooth";
osc.connect(audioContext.destination);
//_____END Setup
//_____BEGIN Switch statement
switch(osc.type) {
case "sawtooth":
osc.frequency.value = 50;
      osc.start(audioContext.currentTime);
break;
case "sine":
osc.frequency.value = 100;
osc.start(audioContext.currentTime);
break;
case "square":
osc.frequency.value = 150;
osc.start(audioContext.currentTime);
break;
default:
osc.frequency.value = 200;
osc.start(audioContext.currentTime);
}
//_____END Switch statement
```

▍ Ternary Operator

If you are writing a conditional statement that contains a single comparison clause (it returns only one of two conditions), then you can use a ternary operator. The ternary operator has three parts: an expression and two executed statements. The first part is an expression that is tested for true or false and is separated from the executed code by a question mark. If the expression evaluates to true, the code to the left of the colon is run. If the expression evaluates to false, the code to the right of the colon is run. The syntax of the ternary operator looks like this:

```
/*
expression ? if true run this code : if false run this code
*/
```

The following code is an example of the ternary operator in action. This code checks if the oscillator type is set to "sawtooth". If it is, the frequency is set to 50; otherwise, it is set to 500.

```
//_____BEGIN setup
let audioContext = new AudioContext();
let osc = audioContext.createOscillator();
osc.type = "sine";
osc.connect(audioContext.destination);
osc.start(audioContext.currentTime);
//_____END setup
//_____BEGIN Ternary example
osc.type === "sawtooth" ? osc.frequency.value = 50 : osc.frequency.
value = 500;
//_____END Ternary example
```

▌ Loops

Computers are very good at doing lots of simple tasks very fast. One of the tools available to leverage this capability is *loops*. Loops allow you to repeat a task until a condition or set of conditions are met. We will cover the following types of loops:

- for

- while

▌ For Loops

The following code is an example of a `for` loop that counts to 16 and outputs each loop number to the console. The text that follows explains the keywords and what each component of the `for` loop does.

```
for(let i = 0; i <=16; i+=1){
  console.log(i)
}
```

A `for` loop consists of the `for` keyword and an opening and closing parenthesis. Inside the parenthesis are three parts separated by semicolons. The first part is the initialization variable, and in this case it is set to 0.

```
for(let i = 0; i <=16; i+=1){
  console.log(i);
}
```

The next part is the conditional statement and is used to determine a condition to check upon each iteration of the loop. As long as this condition is true, the loop will iterate (run another time). In the following example, the condition tells the `for` loop to continue iterating as long as the value of the variable i is less than or equal to 16.

```
for(let i = 0; i <=16; i+=1){
  console.log(i)
}
```

The next part is used to increment the initialization variable. On each loop the variable i is incremented by 1 and eventually reaches 17 and stops looping.

```
for(let i = 0; i <=16; i+=1){
  console.log(i)
}
```

The last part of a for loop is the code block that is defined by the opening and closing curly braces. Any code that is written in between these curly braces gets repeated for each loop iteration.

```
for(let i = 0; i <=16; i+=1){
  console.log(i) // code here gets repeated for each loop
}
```

When for loops are run they are very fast. Below is a script that uses an additional helper function to pause each iteration of a for loop. The loop modifies the frequency of a playing oscillator on each iteration. The helper function pauses the loop (which is its only function) so you can *hear* each change.

```
/*_____BEGIN Helper function.
Ignore this code it is simply being used to pause the for loop */
function sleep(milliseconds) {
let start = new Date().getTime();
for (let i = 0; i < 1e7; i++) {
if ((new Date().getTime() - start) > milliseconds){
break;
}
  }
}
//_____END Helper function
//_____BEGIN Web Audio API setup
let audioContext = new AudioContext();
let osc = audioContext.createOscillator();
osc.type = "sawtooth";
osc.frequency.value = 30;
osc.connect(audioContext.destination);
osc.start(audioContext.currentTime);


//_____END Web Audio API setup
//_____BEGIN audible for-loop example
for(let i =0 ; i < 10; i+=1){
osc.frequency.value +=100;
sleep(500);
}
//_____END audible for-loop example
```

▮ Using For Loops with Arrays

It is common to use loops to modify and extract data from arrays. The following code has an empty array and a for loop. The for loop iterates four times and on each iteration the string "synth" is concatenated with the i variable and is pushed to the synths array. The result is the creation of four entries in the synths array, each consisting of the word "synth" followed by a dash and a number.

```
let synths = [];
    for (let i = 1; i <= 4; i += 1) {
        synths.push("synth-" + i);
}
console.log(synths); //[ 'synth-1', 'synth-2', 'synth-3', 'synth-4' ]
```

If you want to modify each value in an existing array, you can do so by looping through the array and modifying the value at each iteration. To do this, set the value of the conditional statement termination value to the length of the array. In the following code, this is done with synths.length. You can then access the individual values of the array within the loop by placing the iterator variable inside the brackets next to it.

```
let synths = [ 'synth-1', 'synth-2', 'synth-3', 'synth-4' ];
console.log(synths.length); //__This is 4
for (let i = 0; i < synths.length; i += 1) {
console.log(synths[i]);
}
```

The following code shows a modification of the previous code where each value in the array has "0hz" appended to it.

```
let synths = ['synth-1', 'synth-2', 'synth-3', 'synth-4']
for (let i = 0; i < synths.length; i += 1) {
synths[i] += "0hz";
}
console.log(synths); //[ 'synth-10hz', 'synth-20hz', 'synth-30hz',
  'synth-40hz' ]
```

▌▌ While Loops

While loops are useful when you are unsure of how many iterations will be needed to complete a task. A simple analogy might be one of a live podcast website that allows users to connect and listen while a show is on the air. As a programmer, you might not know how long the show will last but you want to continuously check for new user connections for the duration of the show and allow them to listen in. The pseudo code for this analogy might look something like this.

```
let onAir = true;
while(onAir){
// check for new visitors and connect them
}
```

While loops consist of the while keyword, an opening and closing parenthesis, and an opening and closing curly brace. A conditional statement is placed in the parenthesis which allows the loop to iterate as long as the condition remains true. When the condition becomes false, the loop stops. The following example loops

---

as long as the freq variable is greater than zero. At each iteration, the freq variable decrements until it is zero and the loop terminates.

```
let freq = 7000;
while (freq > 0) {
console.log(freq);
freq -= 100;
}
```

When to Use for Loops and When to Use While Loops

The rule of thumb for deciding whether to use a for or while loop is that a for loop is typically used when you know the number of iterations that are needed to complete the loop, and a while loop is used when you don't know how many iterations are needed to complete the loop.

Scope

The concept of scope describes how one part of your program can access variables in another part of your program. To understand scope, you must understand the concept of a code block. A code block is the space in between the curly braces containing executable code such as those used with if statements and for loops.

```
{
}
```

Variables declared with let, const, and var behave differently depending on the context they are declared in.

Block Scoped Variables Using Let and Const

Variables declared using let or const inside a code block are inaccessible by code written outside of that block. This is called *block scope*. For example, the code below contains two variables named osc. The first variable is *not* declared in a code block and is therefore *globally scoped*. The second variable is declared within the if statements curly braces and is therefore *block scoped*. Block scoped variables are said to be *locally scoped* to the statement it is written in; therefore, the second variable is locally scoped to the containing if statement. Even though both variables are named the same thing, they are completely different variables because they are declared in different scopes. Reassigning a value to either variable will not interfere with the other.

```
let osc = 200; // globally scoped variable
if(true){
let osc = 500; // Block scoped!
}
console.log(osc,"The code in the if statement did not change this
variable!"); // 200
```

The same behavior happens when you replace the let keyword with const.

```
const osc = 200; // globally scoped variable
if(true){
const osc = 500; // Block scoped!
}
console.log(osc,"The code in the if statement did not change this
variable!"); // 200
```

■ Non-Block Scoped Variables Using Var

Below is a code example using the var keyword to declare variables. Variables declared with var do not have block scope! These variables have global scope and function scope (you learn about function scope in a future chapter). Variables declared in a (non-function) code block using var are accessible from outside of that code block!

```
var osc = 200; // globally scoped variable
if(true){
var osc = 500; // Globally scoped variable above is changed! Not
block scoped!

}
console.log(osc,"The assignment in the if statement is a reference
to the globally scoped variable!"); // 500
```

■ Local and Higher Scope Access

Code written inside of a code block has access to variables inside *and* outside of the code block. This is true irrespective of the variable declaration keyword you use. The code below contains an if statement that references variables in both the local and global scope.

```
let osc = 200; // globally scoped variable
if(true){
let anotherOsc = 300; // locally scoped variable
console.log(osc); // references the globally scoped variable and
returns 200
console.log(anotherOsc) // references the locally scoped variable
and returns 300
}
```

If a locally declared variable has the same name as a variable in a higher scope, the locally scoped variable takes precedence when being referenced locally.

```
let osc = 200; // globally scoped variable
if(true){
let osc = 300; // locally scoped variable
console.log(osc); // references the locally scoped variable and
returns 300
}
```

▋ Hoisting and Variables

Since the addition of let and const to JavaScript, it is considered bad practice to declare variables using var. However, it is a good idea to understand the behavior of var because you may encounter it when reading code written by other programmers.

When declaring variables with var a behavior called hoisting can create unintended errors in your code. To understand hoisting, you must first understand that variable declaration and initialization are two different things. In the following code, a variable is declared using the var statement and is initialized on the next line.

```
var myData; //_____variable declared
myData = "important data goes here";//__variable initialized
//The following variable is declared and initialized in one line
var playOsc = false;
```

When you declare a variable using var, the JavaScript interpreter immediately (behind the scenes) decouples the declaration from the initialization and moves the variable declaration to the top of the current scope. The following example demonstrates this.

```
hoisting example 1.js
1  test = "the data";
2  var test;
3
4  console.log(test);
5
6
7
8
9
10
11 |
```

```
hoisting example 2.js
1  var test;
2  test = "the data";
3
4  console.log(test);
```

The code on the left contains a variable named test, which is declared *after* it is initialized.

When this code is run, JavaScript changes the order and places the declaration at the top of the current scope, in effect making the code look identical to the code on the right. This is why the test variable is not overwritten when the code is run, even though it appears at first glance that it should be because the variable is not yet declared. Prior to the addition of let and const to JavaScript, it was always considered best practice to declare var prefaced variables at the top of the current scope *because that is where they will be declared anyway.*

It is now considered good practice to only use let and const for variable declarations and to declare variables at the top of the current scope primarily for readability.

▮ Hoisting with Let and Const

Variables declared using let and const are hoisted but remain *uninitialized*. When you attempt to reference a variable created with let or const before it is declared, *you will receive an error.*

As mentioned earlier in the book, the let and const keywords were introduced to JavaScript in 2015 as a way to add block scoped variables to JavaScript. Moving forward, I suggest that you *only* use let and const to declare your variables. Using var is considered bad practice and unnecessary. Throughout the rest of the book, we will not be using var to declare our variables.

▮ Summary

In this chapter, you have learned how to incorporate decision making into your programs using conditional statements. You have also learned how to use loops to accomplish tasks quickly and how they can be leveraged when working with arrays. You learned what block scoped variables are. In the next chapter, you will learn how to incorporate functions into your programs.

---

5 Functions

In this chapter, you will learn about functions, various ways to work with functions, and variable scope while using functions. Functions allow you to write code in a way that avoids repetition. They also allow you to encapsulate your code and perform a specific task based on a set of inputs. You will learn how to use variables in functions when writing programs.

▋ Functions—A Simple Example

To explain functions, let's look at the design of an audio effects module. Imagine a simple hardware audio effects box equipped with a single input channel and a single output channel. Now imagine this effects box *changes* the original input in some way depending on a collection of user-defined settings. In this design, the output of the effects box is the result of the input signal *combined* with the user settings that produce some change in the original signal.

DOI: 10.1201/9781003201496-5

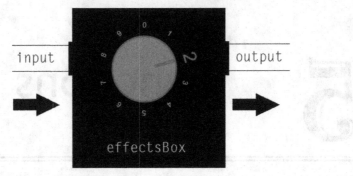

The following example shows how you might code the effects box example for a fixed selection. The `effectsBox` function takes an input, multiplies that input by two, and returns the result.

```
function effectsBox(input) {
return input * 2;
}
console.log(effectsBox(120)); // Output 240
```

The following example shows how you can multiply the input by a value selected by the user, which is coded in the form of a parameter called `multiplier`.

```
function effectsBox(input, multiplier) {
return input * multiplier;
}
console.log(effectsBox(120, 2)); // Output 240
```

▌ Parts of a Function

To create a function, you start by typing the `function` keyword followed by a function name. Immediately following the function name, you place opening and closing parentheses, and then immediately after these you place opening and closing curly braces.

```
function add(){
// function body
}
```

You can give the function placeholders for input values called *parameters*, which you place inside the parentheses and separate by commas.

```
function add(a, b){
}
```

It is considered good practice to name function parameters in a way that reflect their intended inputs. So for example, the function below takes an oscillator type as its first argument and a numeric value as its second argument.

```
function add(oscType, oscValue){
}
```

Commenting parameter inputs is important to ensure that you and other developers know the intended inputs to a function. A common syntax style to describe argument type and its intended use is demonstrated below.

```
/*
@param {string} oscType - an oscillator type such as
square,sine,sawtooth or triangle
@param {number} oscValue - an oscillator value as a number.
*/
function add(oscType, oscValue){
}
```

The final part of a function is an optional return statement that outputs a value when the function completes.

```
function add(a, b){
return a + b;
}
```

To run the function (also called *invoking* the function), you type the function name followed by an opening parenthesis. If the function has parameters, you enter values for these, which in the context of invoking the function are called *arguments*. You end the function with a closing parenthesis.

```
add(2, 5); // 7
```

If you invoke the function with arguments not defined by the function, no error is returned and the system ignores the additional arguments.

```
add(2, 5, 999) //__The third argument is ignored and output is 7
```

▮ Function Expressions

As an alternative to using function declaration syntax, you can write your functions using expression syntax, where you assign the function to a variable like this:

```
let add = function (a,b){
return a + b;
};
add(2,3); // 5
```

The function expression syntax emphasizes an important aspect of JavaScript functions: they can be treated like data and passed around between variables. Here's an example of the previous code with a variable named container that stores the result of running the add function with arguments 2 and 3:

```
let add = function (a, b) {
    return a + b;
};
let container = add(2, 3);
console.log(container); // 5
```

▌ Abstracting Oscillator Playback

The following function `playOsc` plays an oscillator and has two arguments. The first, `oscType`, determines the oscillator waveform type, which for the Web Audio API supports sine, sawtooth, triangle, and square in the form of a string. The second argument is the frequency value in hertz. Because the code necessary to generate the oscillator is encapsulated in a function, you can now invoke the function by writing only one line of code each time you create an oscillator. This means you avoid the repetition of writing out all of the oscillator creation code every time you create the oscillator.

```
const audioContext = new AudioContext(); //___Initializes web audio
api

function playOsc(oscType, freq) {
let osc = audioContext.createOscillator();
osc.type = oscType;
osc.frequency.value = freq; //___freq is a parameter
osc.connect(audioContext.destination);
osc.start(audioContext.currentTime);
}

playOsc("sine", 330); //___Plays oscillator at 330hz



/*___We can play multiple oscillators at once using only
one line of code each time! Adding another sine at 340 will
create a pulsating effect*/



playOsc("sine", 340);
```

▌ A Working Effects Box Example

The following code demonstrates a simplified working example of how an effects box might look when written as a function. The example consists of three functions. The first two functions generate oscillators. The third function is the actual `effectsBox()` function that accepts an oscillator and a filter value as inputs, and then applies the filter to the oscillator.

```
const audioContext = new AudioContext();

//_____BEGIN Custom sound

function customSound(filterVal) {
  let osc_1 = audioContext.createOscillator();
  let filter = audioContext.createBiquadFilter();
  filter.type = "lowpass";
  osc_1.type = "sawtooth";
  osc_1.frequency.value = 300;
  filter.frequency.value = filterVal || filter.frequency.value;
  osc_1.connect(filter);
```

```
    filter.connect(audioContext.destination);
    osc_1.start(audioContext.currentTime);

}

//_____END Custom sound

//_____BEGIN "effectsBox"

function effectsBox(sourceInput, filterParam) {
sourceInput(filterParam);

}

//_____END effectsBox

effectsBox(customSound, 100); // Example
```

▐█ Default Arguments

JavaScript functions allow for default arguments by pre-assigning them as functions parameters. The following function has two default arguments. The first default argument is "sine" and the second is "100".

```
function makeSound(oscType = "sine",oscVal = 100){
    console.log(oscType); // sine
    console.log(oscVal); // 100
}
makeSound(); // sine 100
```

▐█ The Arguments Object

JavaScript contains an array-like object that allows you to access the arguments of a function in the form of a zero-based list. This pseudo-array does not have access to any of the methods of a conventional array *except* the length property. The following code outputs the argument values by specifying the arguments object in console.log().

```
function playOsc(oscType, freq){
  console.log(arguments[0]);
  console.log(arguments[1]);
}
playOsc("sine", 200); // sine 200
```

The arguments object can be combined with the length property and a conditional statement to ensure that an error is given if any arguments are left empty. To create your own error statement, you use the throw keyword. In the following code, the conditional statement checks to see if the number of arguments is *not* two, and if the conditional statement evaluates to true, then an error is given (or *thrown*) to indicate this result.

```
function playOsc(oscType,freq){
```

```
if(arguments.length !==2){
throw "Error! This function takes two arguments"
}
}
playOsc("sine") //___Error! This function takes two arguments
```

You can add another check to ensure that the correct data types are being entered like this:

```
function playOsc(oscType, freq) {
  if (arguments.length !== 2) {
      throw "Error! This function takes two arguments";
  }
  //_____Check for correct argument data types
  if (typeof oscType !== "string" || typeof freq !== "number") {
      throw "Please enter the correct argument types";
  }
}
playOsc(100, true); //___Please enter the correct argument types
```

▮ Rest Parameter

The rest parameter lets you create functions that have an undefined number of parameters. The rest parameter also gives you access all arguments of a function as an array. Unlike the arguments object, the rest parameter returns a real array that responds to JavaScript's built-in array methods. Using comments to document the intended inputs of a function is more important when using the rest parameter because unlike a conventional function, the parameters are not named individually.

```
function doThing(...allArgs){
  console.log(allArgs)
}
doThing("one","two","three"); // [ 'one', 'two', 'three' ]
```

▮ Function Scope

Scope defines how one part of a program can access variables in another part of a program. JavaScript's original design had two forms of scope and these are global scope and function scope. With the introduction of block scoping, scope is extended to parts of the language other than functions such as loops and conditional statements. Functions are still the primary building block in JavaScript used to encapsulate different parts of your program. This means that if you declare a variable within a function, it is specific to *that* function and does not conflict with any other variables that have the same name and are defined outside of that function. Functions have access to their own variables and they also have access to any variables in a *higher* scope, which includes the global scope.

In one of our previous examples, we created a function to play an oscillator. Notice that although the audioContext variable is not included inside the playOsc function, it is still accessible. This is because audioContext is defined in a higher scope: the global scope.

```
//____audioContext is global
const audioContext = new AudioContext();
//____ playOsc has access to it
function playOsc(oscType, freq){
let osc = audioContext.createOscillator();
osc.type = oscType;
osc.frequency.value = freq; //____freq is a parameter
osc.connect(audioContext.destination);
osc.start(audioContext.currentTime);
}
playOsc("sine", 330);//____Plays oscillator at 330hz
```

You can use function scope to protect variables defined in a function not only from variables defined in a higher scope but also from variables defined in other functions. In the following example, there are two functions. One *has* data, and the other *wants* data. The data of the first function is *not* accessible to the other function because it is hidden in a local scope.

```
function iHaveData() {
  let data = "The data";  // <-- this variable......
}
function iWantData() {
  return data;            // <-- is not accessible here...
}
iWantData(); // data is not defined
```

If you declare two variables with the same name and one is globally scoped (or in a higher scope) and the other is locally scoped within a function, the locally scoped variable is referenced when the code in the function is running.

So, for example, in the following code, the multFreq function takes a single argument and multiplies it by a value that is assigned to the multiplier variable. The globally scoped multiplier is not referenced when multFreq() is running because the function has a locally scoped variable with the same name.

```
let multiplier = 4; //_____This variable is not referenced by
multFreq
function multFreq(frequency) {
  let multiplier = 2; //____because this one has the same name and
  is locally scoped!
  return frequency * multiplier;
}
console.log(multFreq(200)); // 400
console.log(multiplier); // 4
```

If the locally scoped multiplier variable declaration inside the previous function is removed, then during function execution, the code will look outside the function for a variable with the referenced name.

```
let multiplier = 4;
function multFreq(frequency) {
/*__There is no local multiplier variable so it finds one in the
scope above it__*/
return frequency * multiplier;
```

```
}
console.log(multFreq(200)); // 800
```

▉ Why You Should Always Declare Your Variables

In JavaScript, the use of global variables should generally be kept to a minimum. This is because when programs get large, the accumulation of global variables increases the likelihood of naming collisions. Typically, this is not a problem for small applications. However, when programs begin to grow, they will usually incorporate libraries and third-party scripts that depend on some global variables. Accidentally overwriting these global variables can cause your program to break.

When you declare a variable from within a function *without* a declaration statement, the variable is referenced from the global scope when the function is invoked. This can have the side effect of overwriting a preexisting global variable with the same name and creating an unexpected name collision. The following code demonstrates how this can happen.

The following example contains a global variable named `multiplier`. There is also a variable named `multiplier` inside of the `multFreq` function that is not declared using the let or const keywords. When the function is invoked, the `multiplier` variable references the global `multiplier` variable, changing its value from 4 to 2! This is an example of why you should *always* remember to declare your variables with a declaration keyword such as let or const.

```
let multiplier = 4;
function multFreq(frequency) {
multiplier = 2; //_____Notice no let or const declaration!
return frequency * multiplier;
}
console.log(multFreq(200)); // 400
console.log(multiplier); //____Changed to 2!
```

▉ Hoisting and Functions

We explained in the previous chapter how hoisting affects variables. In addition to affecting variables, hoisting also affects functions. And hoisting works differently based on whether the function is written with declaration or expression syntax.

Consider the following function declaration. In this code, the function is invoked *before* it is declared, yet it still works! This is because behind the scenes, the declaration is hoisted to the top of the scope, which allows you to execute the function even though it is not yet declared.

```
multFreq(200, 2); /*__This still works even though it is invoked
before it is declared!_*/
function multFreq(input, val) {
    return input * val;
}
```

The following example of the same function written using expression syntax, however, throws an error. This happens because function expressions are treated like variables, with the declaration being hoisted to the top. Remember that the initialization of the variable still happens where the variable is initialized in the code. In this case, the function is run before the initialization that defines the function occurs. The lesson here is that when you use function expressions, you must declare functions before you invoke them. This is good practice with all your functions as it makes your code less confusing and more readable.

```
multFreq(200, 2); // ___ error! "multFreq is not a function".
let multFreq = function(input, val) {
return input * val
}
let multFreq = function(input, val) { // declaration before
invocation!
return input * val
}
multFreq(200, 2);  // works as expected
```

▮ Anonymous Functions

Anonymous functions are functions that do not have a name. Technically, the function in the following code is an anonymous function because the variable it is assigned to is not the function name. It is the container name for an anonymous function.

```
let multFreq = function(input, val) {
return input * val
}
  To give this function a name, you do it like this:

let multFreq = function nameGoesHere(input, val) {
return input * val
}
```

Note, however, that to invoke the function, you use the variable name that it is assigned to.

```
multFreq(100,2) // 200
```

In JavaScript, it is possible to create a function that is invoked immediately after it is declared. This type of function is called an *immediately invoked function expression* or IIFE (pronounced "iffy"). This method is useful if you want to briefly encapsulate and run a block of code only once. The syntax looks like this:

```
//_____BEGIN IIFE
(function run() {
return "data";
}());
//_____END IIFE
```

To view the output, you can wrap it in `console.log()`.

```
console.log(
//_____BEGIN IIFE
(function run() {
return "data";
}())
//_____END IIFE
);
```

The first thing to notice is that the function is wrapped in parentheses. This is optional, but is considered best practice because it helps differentiate the construct syntactically from non-IIFE functions.

```
(function run() {
  return "data";
}());
```

The next thing to notice is the parentheses toward the end of the function before the closing, encapsulating parenthesis. This syntax is what invokes the function.

```
(function run() {
  return "data";
}());
```

To add parameters and arguments, you put parameters in the first set of parentheses and arguments in the second set of parentheses.

```
(function add(a, b) { //_____ parameters
  return a + b;
}(2, 3)); //_____arguments
```

▌ Closures

One of the most difficult aspects of the JavaScript language for new programmers to grasp is closures. Understanding closures will ultimately allow you to write cleaner code while giving you a powerful tool to solve a host of problems you will inevitably run into. Understanding the concept of closure can be a bit difficult at first. But in the long term, the benefits are worth the time investment.

▌ What Is a Closure?

A closure is an inner function that has access to the scope of its outer environment even after that outer environment has returned. To understand what this means, you must first solidify your understanding of scope. The following example demonstrates how a function has access to its local scope, the global scope, and its local arguments.

```
let globalVariable = "global variable";
function doSomething(argInput) {
```

```
            let localVariable = "local variable";
            lconsole.log(argInput);
            lconsole.log(globalVariable);
            lconsole.log(localVariable);
}
doSomething("argument input"); /*_____This outputs: "argument
input" "global variable" "local variable" */
because the function has access to its own scope and the outer scope.*/
```

If a function is defined inside another function, it too has access to the data of the container function, as well as its own locally scoped variables. In the following example, testScope() is a container function for innerFunction().

```
let globalVariable = "global variable";
function testScope(argInput) {
        let testScopeLocalVariable = "local variable from testScope";
            //____The inner function has access to everything
    outside of it
        function innerFunction() {
        let localVariable = "local variable from innerFunction";
        console.log(argInput);
        console.log(globalVariable);
        console.log(testScopeLocalVariable);
        console.log(localVariable);


}


        innerFunction();
}


testScope("argument input");


/*The console logs:
"argument input"
"global variable"
"local variable from testScope"
"local variable from innerFunction"
*/
```

As we mentioned, a closure is an inner function that has access to the scope of its outer environment *even after that outer environment has returned*. The previous examples demonstrated scope access. The following example demonstrates what it means for a function to have scope access even after the outer environment has returned. The outer environment can be either the global environment or another function. The following code includes the effectsBox function that contains a single variable named component. The effectsBox function returns a function that returns the value of component. When the initial effectsBox function is invoked, it returns a function declaration named openEffectsBox to the outer scope (in this case the global scope). This openEffectsBox function declaration is then assigned to a variable called getComponent, which is then invoked and returns the string "Pulled out component".

The important thing to realize here is that a closure (the inner function) can return data (such as the component variable) from its containing environment [in this case effectsBox()] even after that outer environment [effects-Box()] has returned.

```
function effectsBox() {
  let component = "Pulled out component";
  return function openEffectsBox() {
    return component;
  };
}
let getComponent = effectsBox(); //___stores "openEffectsBox"
function in a variable.
console.log(getComponent()); // "Pulled out component"
```

The previous example can be modified to demonstrate how *state can be modified and retained* using the closure. In this code, there is an additional counter variable that increments each time the inner openEffectsBox function is invoked. Since closures allow access to the scope of a containing function even after that containing function has returned, the returned function can continue to increment the counter variable and have access to its state.

```
function effectsBox() {
  let counter = 0;
  let component = "Pulled out component";
  return function openEffectsBox() {
    return component + " " + (counter += 1);
  };
}
let getComponent = effectsBox(); //___stores "openEffectsBox"
function in a variable.


getComponent(); // "Pulled out component 1"
getComponent(); // "Pulled out component 2"
getComponent(); // "Pulled out component 3"
getComponent(); // "Pulled out component 4"
```

Here is an example of a function designed to play an oscillator by returning an inner function that remembers the outer environment's state. This example shows how the inner function accesses the function arguments of the outer function even after the outer function returns. The playOsc function takes parameter type, whereas the inner function it returns takes parameter freq. The outer function is invoked with the argument "sine"; thereafter, the inner function is invoked with a frequency value. The result is a sine wave that plays at a set frequency value of 140 Hz.

```
const audioContext = new AudioContext();


function playOsc(type) {
  return function(freq) {
```

```
        let osc = audioContext.createOscillator();
        osc.type = type;
        osc.frequency.value = freq;
    osc.connect(audioContext.destination);
    osc.start(audioContext.currentTime);
  };
}
let sinewave = playOsc("sine");
sinewave(140); //_____Plays sine wave at 140 hz
```

Closure is an advanced concept that can be used to protect a portion of a program from the global scope, retain state, and organize your code. Its specific use cases will gradually become more apparent as your skill as a programmer develops. For now, it is important to grasp what a closure is.

▌ Callback Functions

A `callback` is a function that is used as an argument to another function. The following example demonstrates addition of two numbers using a callback.

```
function doMath(callback) {
  return callback();

}
function addTwoNumbers() {
  return 2 + 2;
}
doMath(addTwoNumbers); // 4
```

When working with callbacks, you will often see function invocations where the callback declaration is placed directly in a function argument.

```
function doStuff(callback) {
  return callback();
}



doStuff(function() { // ___Callback declaration is used directly
  return //___data
});
```

The following function is an example of using a callback to make a function more flexible. The `calculateFrequencies` function is designed to take three arguments. The first two are numbers and the third is a callback that manipulates the other arguments. If the user does not use a callback, then the function defaults to multiplying the two arguments together.

```
function calculateFrequencies(a, b, callback) {
if (callback === undefined) {
    return a * b;
} else {
    return callback(a, b);
```

```
}
}
function diff(a, b) {
    return Math.abs(a - b);
}
console.log(calculateFrequencies(200, 2));// 400___Multiplies
numbers
console.log(calculateFrequencies(1000, 4000, diff));//  3000___uses
custom callback to find the difference
```

The previous example demonstrates how passing a callback to a function provides the *action* taken by the callback, whereas passing nonfunction values provides *data* input.

Array Method	Description
filter()	Compares each element in an array to a conditional statement and returns a new array of elements that meet the condition
map()	Calls a function on each element in an array and returns a new array with the mapped value of each element in the input array

▋ Working with JavaScript's Built-In Callback Functions

Learning to design your own functions that use callbacks is an advanced topic. As a beginner, the more important thing for you to know is how to use preexisting methods that have been designed to use callbacks. The following are two examples of built-in JavaScript methods that use callbacks to help you work with arrays.

▋ filter()

The `filter` method compares each element in an array to a conditional statement and returns a new array of only those elements that meet the filter condition. The following example uses `filter()` to loop through an array of frequency values to create a new array of values greater than or equal to 1000.

```
let freq1 = 1200,
freq2 = 570,
freq3 = 100,
freq4 = 1500;

let frequencyList = [freq1, freq2, freq3, freq4];
let filteredFrequencies = frequencyList.filter(function(value) {
    return value >= 1000;
});

console.log(filteredFrequencies); //___ [1200,1300]
```

▐ map()

The map function calls a function on each element in an array and returns a new array that contains the mapped data for each element in the input array.

The following example uses map() to add 100 to each value in an array and return a new array named newFreqs.

```
let freqs = [100, 200, 300];
let newFreqs = freqs.map(function (val) {
    return val + 100;
});
console.log(newFreqs); //__ [ 200, 300, 400 ]
```

The callback functions of both map() and filter() take three arguments. In order of their position, these are value, index, and array. The value argument is the array value at the current index, the index argument is the current index value, and the array argument is the array that the callback is being applied to. In the following example, a map method is applied to an array and all three arguments are logged to the console.

```
let freqs = [100, 200, 300];
let newFreqs = freqs.map(function(val, index, arr) {
    let message = "current value: " + val + " current index index:
" + index + " array: " + arr;
    console.log(message);
    return val;
});
/*__This logs the following to the console
current value: 100 current index: 0 array: 100,200,300
current value: 200 current index: 1 array: 100,200,300
current value: 300 current index: 2 array: 100,200,300
*/
```

▐ Function Arrow Syntax

When writing callbacks it is a common convention to use an alternative syntax called *arrow* syntax. Arrow syntax is considered easier to read and more concise. Below are two filter functions, one uses the conventional callback syntax and the other uses arrow syntax.

```
let freqs = [100, 200, 300];
// Conventional callback syntax.
let newFreqs = freqs.map(function (val) {
    return val + 100;
});

console.log(newFreqs); //__ [ 200, 300, 400 ]
// // Arrow syntax
let freqs = [100, 200, 300];
let newFreqs = freqs.map((val) => {
    return val + 100;
});
console.log(newFreqs); //__ [ 200, 300, 400 ]
```

To convert a conventional callback to an arrow function you remove the function keyword and place an arrow operator to the right of the parenthesis. An arrow operator looks like the following example.

```
=>
```

A conventional callback function looks like this:

```
function(){}
```

The arrow function version is rewritten to look like this:

```
()=>{}
```

Arrow syntax can be made more concise if the callback only has a single argument. In such a case the parenthesis can be removed.

```
let freqs = [100, 200, 300];
let newFreqs = freqs.map(val => {   // argument parenthesis removed
  return val + 100;
});
```

If the callback function is only used to return a value and does not contain code in the body, the return statement and curly braces can be removed as well.

```
let freqs = [100, 200, 300];
let newFreqs = freqs.map(val => val + 100); // argument
parenthesis, return statement and curly braces removed.
```

Arrow functions are commonly used as a replacement for function expressions.
An example of a function expression converted to an arrow function is demonstrated below.

```
// Conventional function expression syntax
let add = function (valOne,valTwo){
    let result = valOne + valTwo;
    return result
}
console.log(add(2,3)) // 5

// Arrow syntax version
let add = (valOne,valTwo) => {
  let result = valOne + valTwo;
  return result
}
console.log(add(2,3)) // 5
```

Typically, if a function expression does not contain a body of code and is only used to return a value, it is written like the following example.

```
let add = (valOne,valTwo) => valOne + valTwo;
console.log(add(2,3));  // 5
```

Recursion

Recursion is an advanced programming topic, and it will only be explored briefly in this chapter.

A recursive function is a function that calls itself. The following is an example of a recursive function.

```
function x(){
return x()
}
```

If you run the previous code, it will crash your browser. This is because, when a recursive function runs indefinitely, it eventually uses up the resources of your code interpreter (in this case the web browser) and creates an error. To use recursion effectively, you need to set a condition to terminate the recursion. This condition is called the *base case*.

The following example is a recursive function named `loopFromTo` that contains a working base case. `loopFromTo` takes two arguments, and both are numbers. In the function body, a conditional statement is used to check if the argument named `start` is less than the argument named `end`. As long as this condition is true, `loopFromTo` calls itself and on each iteration increments the `start` argument by one. This continues until the recursion terminates when `start` ceases to be less than `end` and the conditional statement evaluates to false.

```
function loopFromTo(start, end) {
console.log(start);
if (start < end) {
    return loopFromTo(start += 1, end)
}
}


loopFromTo(1, 8) //_____ 1,2,3,4,5,6,7,8
```

Recursive functions can be used in place of looping constructs and are an invaluable tool in many complex algorithms. If recursion seems confusing don't worry, you can program perfectly good applications while you become familiar with it.

Summary

In this chapter, you learned how to create and use functions. In the next chapter, you will expand your understanding of JavaScript to include a concept called object-oriented programming.

6   Objects

So far, we discussed six of JavaScript's eight data types. These are string, number, Boolean, undefined, BigInt, and null. These are called *primitive data types*. Anything that is not a primitive data type is of the *object* data type. In the previous chapter, you learned about functions, which are of the object data type. In this chapter, you will learn how to program using object literals, which are also of the object data type.

▮▮ JavaScript Data Types

The JavaScript data types are:

- String

- Number

- Boolean

- Undefined

- Null

DOI: 10.1201/9781003201496-6

- Object

- BigInt

- Symbol

The object data type includes functions, arrays, and object literals. Arrays and functions have already been explored, so here is a general definition of object literals: Object literals are a collection of comma-separated key-value pairs that are contained within curly braces.

> *Note: Developers in the JavaScript world commonly refer to object literals as objects. However, object literals and the object data type are two different things. One way to understand the difference is to recognize that the object data type is a category that contains object literals, functions, and arrays.*

In the following code, an object named `obj` is created and the values within curly braces are assigned to it.

```
let obj = {
  key1: "value1",
  key2: "value2"
};
```

A key is similar to a variable, and a value is similar to the data assigned to a variable. The key and value of an object is called a *property* for nonfunctions assigned to a key, or a *method* for functions assigned to a key.

```
let obj = {
  key: "value", //___This is a property
  doSomething: function(){ //___This is a method
  }
};
```

Another syntax for creating methods is demonstrated below. The syntax works identically to the code above.

```
let obj = {
  key: "value", //___This is a property
  doSomething(){ //___This is a method with a more concise working
syntax
  }
};
```

Conceptually, object literals are used to model real-world elements in your code. So, for example, the following object is used to model a music album.

```
//_____This is an object that contains album
datalet album = {
```

```
    name:"Thriller Funk",
    artist:"James Jackson",
    format:"wave",
    sampleRate:44100
}
```

To access data from an object, you can use dot notation, which looks like this:

```
album.name; // Thriller Funk
album.artist; // James Jackson
album.format; // wave
album.sampleRate; // 44100
```

Alternatively, you can use bracket notation to access values in an object.

```
album["sampleRate"]; // 44100
```

If you use a bracket notation, you must type the key in the form of a string.
```
album[
"sampleRate"
];
```

//__The key is a string
You can use methods to modify or retrieve data from an object. Here is an example of an object that contains a method that returns the name and artist information of an object named *song*.

```
let song = {
  name: "Funky Shuffle",
  artist: "James Jackson",
  format: "wave",
  sampleRate: 44100,
  //_____BEGIN Method
    nameAndArtist() {
      return "Name: " + song.name + " | " + "Artist: " + song.
artist
    }
  //_____END Method
}
```

You can invoke methods with dot notation and trailing parentheses.

```
//_____BEGIN method invocation
song.nameAndArtist(); // Name: Funky Shuffle| Artist: James Jackson
//_____END method invocation
```

▮ Looping through Objects

To loop through the keys and values of an object, you use a for in loop. You code a for in loop like this:

```
let song = {
  name: "Funky Shuffle",
  artist: "James Jackson",
```

```
    format: "wave",
    sampleRate: 44100
}
//_____BEGIN for in loop
for (let prop in song) {
  console.log(prop + ":"); //__Outputs each key
  console.log(song[prop]); //__Outputs each value
}
//_____END for in loop
```

The structure of a for in loop consists of the for keyword followed by a variable that represents the value of each property. In the previous example, this variable was named prop. The variable name is followed by the in keyword and the name of the object you want to loop through.

Often you will want to modify the properties of an object you are looping through while not modifying any of its methods. One way you can do this is by using a conditional statement and the *typeof* operator to act only on property values that are *not* functions. This usage is shown in the following code:

```
let song = {
  name: "Funky Shuffle",
  artist: "James Jackson",
  format: "wave",
  sampleRate: 44100,
  nameAndArtist() {
    return "Name: " + song.name + " | " + "Artist: " + song.artist;
  }
};
for (let prop in song) {
  if (typeof song[prop] !== "function") {
    console.log(song[prop]); //___Omits methods
  }
}
```

▌▌ When to Use Objects Rather than Arrays

You have probably noticed that objects and arrays are similar because they allow you to organize collections of data. If you are curious about when to use an array rather than an object, the rule of thumb is that if the order of the data matters, you should *always* use an array. The reason for this is that there is nothing in the JavaScript specification that guarantees the order in which key-value pairs of an object are returned in a loop.

▌▌ How to Check If an Object Has Access to a Particular Property or Method

If you want to check whether a property or method is available to an object, you can use the in operator.

```
let song = {
```

```
  name: "Funky Shuffle",
  artist: "James Jackson",
  getArtist() {
    return song.artist;
  }
};
console.log("artist" in song); //true
console.log("getArtist" in song); //true
```

▐ Cloning Objects

If you want to create an object that has access to another object's properties and methods, while being extensible, you can use the Object.create() function. The following example shows an object being cloned using this method.

```
let effect = {
  type:"reverb",
  value:"50%"
};


let newEffect = Object.create(effect);
newEffect.type = "reverb";
console.log(newEffect) // {type: "reverb" value:"50%"}
```

You can then extend the newly created object with properties and methods.

```
newEffect.fuzz = "20%";
newEffect.drive = "10%";
```

The newly created object is now a combination of original properties, overwritten properties, and new properties. The newEffect object looks like the following:

```
{ type: 'distortion',value:"50%",fuzz: '20%', drive: '10%' }
```

Performing console.log(newEffect) will log the code to the browser, use the arrow icons to see all properties and methods of the object.

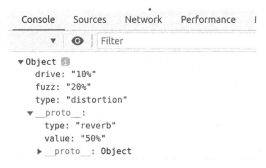

▌▌ Prototypal Inheritance

It is important to understand that Object.create() does not literally copy the properties and methods to a new object but provides a reference to the properties and methods contained in the parent object(s). This hierarchy of references between objects is called *prototypal inheritance*. The following code shows this by cloning multiple objects and including comments of the hierarchy of property accessibility.

```
let synth = {
    name: "Moog",
    polyphony: 32
};
let synthWithFilters = Object.create(synth); //clone synth

//synthWithFilters now has access to name and polyphony properties
synthWithFilters.filters = ["lowpass", "highpass", "bandpass"]; //
add property

/*The original synth object does not have access to the filters
property. */
let synthWithFiltersAndEffects = Object.create(synthWithFilters);
//clone synthWithFilters

synthWithFiltersAndEffects.effects = ["reverb", "flange","chorus"];
//add property
/*Neither the synth object nor the synthWithFilters object have
access to the effects property*/
```

▌▌ Object.creates Nested Object Gotcha

When properties of a prototype object are assigned other objects, it creates a potential problem if the prototype is cloned using Object.create. The problem is that when you change any properties of the cloned object that *are* objects, the original prototype is changed as well.

```
let synth = {

    name: "Moog",              •

    polyphony: 32,

    filters: {lowpass:80, highPass:5000}

};

let newSynth = Object.create(synth);
newSynth.name = "Roland";
console.log(synth.name) // this does not change and remains "Moog".
// however, watch this!
newSynth.filters.lowpass = 150;
newSynth.filters.highpass = 10000;

// The original is changed!
console.log(synth.filters) // { lowpass: 150, highpass: 10000}
```

This behavior is duplicated with arrays because arrays are of the object data type.

```
let synth = {
    name: "Moog",
    polyphony: 32,
    filters: ["lowpass", "highpass", "bandpass"]
}
let newSynth = Object.create(synth);
newSynth.name = "Roland";
console.log(synth.name) // this does not change and remains "Moog".
// however, watch this!
newSynth.filters[0] = "comb";
// The original is changed!
console.log(synth.filters) // [ 'comb', 'highpass', 'bandpass']
```

When using `Object.create` the returned object is referred to as a *shallow copy*. To get around the aforementioned problem of keeping your original objects free from change when copying them, you need to create a *deep copy*. An object that is a deep copy does not reference a prototype and all values are copied directly to the new object. Unfortunately, as of this writing JavaScript does not have an easy way to create deep object copies and to do so requires developers to write a custom algorithm. Below is a function to create deep copied objects and a demonstration of its usage. I've included this code here to assure you that there is a solution to the deep copy/shallow copy problem. We don't expect you to understand how the code below works just yet! At this point, you should be able to use the below code and run the function irrespective of understanding how its internals work.

```
//@param {obj} original - an object to copy.
function deepCopy (obj) {
    let _out = new obj.constructor;
    let getType = function (n) {
        return Object.prototype.toString.call(n).slice(8, -1);
    }
    for (let _key in obj) {
        if (obj.hasOwnProperty(_key)) {
            _out[_key] = getType(obj[_key]) === 'Object' ||
getType(obj[_key]) === 'Array' ? deepCopy(obj[_key]) : obj[_key];
        }
    }
    return _out;
}
// example usage
let synth = {
    name: "Moog",
    polyphony: 32,
    filters: {lowpass:80, highPass:5000}
};
let synthTwo = deepCopy(synth);
synthTwo.filters.bandPass = 2000;
console.log(synth.filters); // does not change { lowpass: 80,
highPass: 5000 }
console.log(synthTwo.filters); // updated as expected { lowpass:
80, highPass: 5000, bandPass: 2000 }
```

■ The "this" Keyword

JavaScript contains a keyword called this that is used in methods to refer to an object. In the following code, the method named nameAndArtist references its containing object directly by using its name, which is song.

```
let song = {
  name: "Funky Shuffle",
  artist: "James Jackson",
  format: "wave",
  sampleRate: 44100,
  //_____BEGIN Method
  nameAndArtist() {
    return "Name: " + song.name + " | " + "Artist:" + song.
artist;  }
  //_____END Method
};
The reference to song can be replaced with the this keyword, and
the result is the same.
let song = {
  name: "Funky Shuffle",
  artist: "James Jackson",
  format: "wave",
  sampleRate: 44100,
  //_____BEGIN Method
  nameAndArtist() {
    return "Name: " + this.name + " | " + "Artist:" + this.artist;
  }
  //_____END Method
};
console.log(song.nameAndArtist()) // Funky Shuffle | Artist:James
Jackson
```

■ The bind Function

The usefulness of the this keyword becomes apparent when you realize that *any function or method can be applied to any object*. The easiest way to demonstrate this is by using the built-in JavaScript method called bind. The bind method points a function's this value to the object specified in the first argument (the *bound* object). You can then invoke the function on the *bound* object. In the following code, bind points the getName function's this value to an object named album.

```
let song = {
  name: "Funky Shuffle",
  artist: "James Jackson",
  format: "wave",
  sampleRate: 44100
};
function getName() {
  return this.name;
}
let getNameOfSong = getName.bind(song); /*assign bound function to
  a variable*/
```

```
//_____Then invoke it!
console.log(getNameOfSong()); // Funky Shuffle
```

If you want to specify arguments in a function created with bind, you can do this in one of two ways. The first is to specify the arguments in the newly created function. In the following example, a function named descriptor is invoked on an object named blastSound. An argument is then passed to the describe-BlastSound function.

```
let blastSound = {
  name: "Blast"
};
function descriptor(message) {
  return this.name + "! " + message;
}
let describeBlastSound = descriptor.bind(blastSound);
console.log(describeBlastSound("This is an explosive sound"));
  //Blast: This is an explosive sound
```

Alternatively, you can specify the arguments in the statement where you bind the function to the object. You do this by first specifying the object to bind to, then specifying arguments you want to use and separating them with commas, as in the following example:

```
let describeBlastSound = descriptor.bind(blastSound, "This is an
  explosive sound");
console.log(describeBlastSound()); /*Blast: This is an explosive
  sound*/
```

As you can see, even when a function has not been written as a method on a particular object, you can still apply the function to that object. This also means that you can use a method of one object and apply it to a completely different object. The following code uses a method named getNameAndArtist of an object named song and applies it to an object named album.

```
let album = {
  name: "Funky Shuffle",
  artist: "James Jackson",
  format: "wave",
  sampleRate: 44100
};
let song = {
  name: "Analogue Heaven",
  artist: "The Keep It Reels",
  getNameAndArtist() {
    return "Name: " + this.name + " | Artist: " + this.artist;  }
};
let getNameOfAlbum = song.getNameAndArtist.bind(album);
console.log(getNameOfAlbum()); /*Name: Funky Shuffle | Artist:
  James Jackson*/
```

If a function is invoked outside the context of an object, its this value points to one of two values, depending on whether strict mode is used or not. If strict mode is used, its this value is undefined. If strict mode is not used, its this value points to an invisible object called the *global* object, which contains all the built-in properties and methods of the web browser. You can view the value of this by using console.log(this) in the global scope without strict mode.

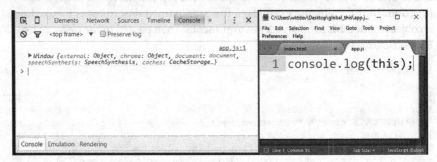

▌ Summary

In this chapter, you learned how to program with objects. In the next chapter, you will learn the basics of the Web Audio API node graph and working with oscillators.

7 Node Graphs and Oscillators

In previous chapters, you learned the basics of working with JavaScript data types and how to use the Web Audio API to generate basic tones. In this chapter, you will use your understanding of JavaScript to get a better understanding of two core features of the Web Audio API: node graphs and oscillators.

▮ The `AudioContext()` Method

The Web Audio API is accessed by using a collection of properties and methods of an object that you create using the `AudioContext()` method.

```
const AudioContext = new AudioContext();
```

`AudioContext()` is a constructor that returns an object when you use the keyword new. Constructors and the new keyword are explained in Chapter 12. For now, the important thing to understand is that `AudioContext()` returns an object containing all of the methods and properties that you use to access the Web Audio API.

▌ Node Graphs

A node graph is a collection of nodes. A node in a node graph is an object that represents an audio input source, such as an oscillator, or an object designed to manipulate an audio input source such as a filter. These nodes are connected together using a method named `connect`.

The following code is an example of an oscillator node connected to a filter node.

```
"use strict";
const   audioContext = new AudioContext();
//_____BEGIN create oscillator and filter
let filter = audioContext.createBiquadFilter();
let oscillator = audioContext.createOscillator();
//_____END create oscillator and filter
//_____BEGIN connect oscillator to filter
oscillator.connect(filter);
//_____END connect oscillator to filter
//_____BEGIN connect filter to computer speakers
filter.connect(audioContext.destination);
//_____END connect filter to computer speakers
//_____BEGIN start oscillator playing
oscillator.start(audioContext.currentTime);
//_____END start oscillator playing
```

In the previous code, the oscillator object is created using the `createOscillator` method of the audio context and stored in a variable named `oscillator`. You create the filter object in a similar way by invoking the `createBiquadFilter` method of `audioContext`. The `oscillator` is connected to the filter using `connect()`. The `filter` is connected to a property named `destination`. The `destination` represents the output of your computer's audio system. To start the oscillator playing, you use a method of the `oscillator` object named `start`. The `start` method takes one argument that determines the time the oscillator starts playing. The value of `audioContext.currentTime` is the current time in seconds within the Web Audio API, starting when `AudioContext` was invoked. (The topic of time is discussed in Chapter 21.)

▌ Oscillators

Oscillators, like all Web Audio API nodes, have their own custom properties and methods. The following methods and properties are discussed in this chapter:

Method	Description
start	Starts oscillator playing
stop	Stops oscillator playing

Property	Description
onended	Executes a custom function when oscillator stops
type	Sets the type of waveform assigned to the oscillator
frequency	Sets the frequency value of the oscillator in hertz
detune	Sets an offset of the current frequency value in cents

∎ The stop Method

The stop method determines when an oscillator stops. It takes one numeric argument that represents a time value in seconds. The following code starts an oscillator playing and stops it 3 seconds into the future:

```
let  audioContext = new AudioContext();
let oscillator = audioContext.createOscillator();
oscillator.connect(audioContext.destination);
oscillator.start(audioContext.currentTime);
oscillator.stop(audioContext.currentTime + 3);
```

∎ The onended Property

If you want to launch a function after the oscillator stop method has run, you assign that function to the onended property. The following code outputs the string "Oscillator has stopped" to the console after its stop method completes.

```
const  audioContext = new AudioContext();
let oscillator = audioContext.createOscillator();
oscillator.connect(audioContext.destination);
oscillator.start(audioContext.currentTime);
oscillator.stop(audioContext.currentTime + 3);
oscillator.onended = function() {
  console.log("Oscillator has stopped");
};
```

∎ How to Stop Oscillators and Restart Them

When an oscillator is stopped, it cannot be restarted. Instead, it must be recreated and then started. To demonstrate this, the following code attempts to restart an oscillator after it has stopped, which results in failure.

```
const AudioContext = new AudioContext();
let oscillator = audioContext.createOscillator();
oscillator.connect(audioContext.destination);
oscillator.start(audioContext.currentTime);
oscillator.stop(audioContext.currentTime + 3);
oscillator.onended = function() {
  oscillator.start(audioContext.currentTime); // fails!
};
```

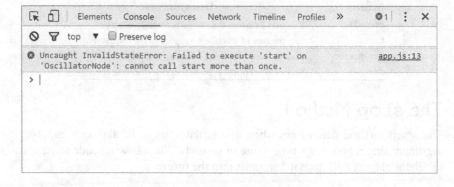

The following code recreates an oscillator and starts it playing 1 second after the previous oscillator stops.

```
let oscillator = audioContext.createOscillator();
oscillator.connect(audioContext.destination);
oscillator.start(audioContext.currentTime);
oscillator.stop(audioContext.currentTime + 3);
oscillator.onended = function() {
  oscillator = audioContext.createOscillator();
  oscillator.connect(audioContext.destination);
  oscillator.start(audioContext.currentTime + 1); /*start in
    one second*/
};
```

▌ The `type` Property

The `type` property of an oscillator sets its waveform type in the form of a string. There are four predefined waveform shapes available.

- sawtooth

- sine

- square

- triangle

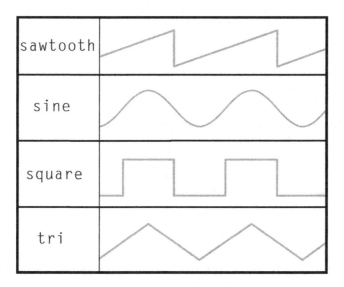

You assign a waveform type to an oscillator like this:

```
const AudioContext = new AudioContext();
let oscillator = audioContext.createOscillator();
oscillator.connect(audioContext.destination);
oscillator.type = "sawtooth";
oscillator.start(audioContext.currentTime);
```

The default waveform type is sine.

▌ The `frequency` Property

To set an oscillator's frequency, you must set the frequency property to a number. The frequency value is represented in hertz.

```
const AudioContext = new AudioContext();
let oscillator = audioContext.createOscillator();
oscillator.connect(audioContext.destination);
oscillator.frequency.value = 80; //    80 hertz
oscillator.start(audioContext.currentTime);
```

▌ The `detune` Property

The detune property is expressed in cents. In the Western music scale, there are 100 cents per half-step note. This makes it easy to create musical note relationships using detune. The following code plays a note at a frequency of 130.81 Hz and is the frequency of a C3 note. The oscillator stops, and a half-second later a second note plays with the same frequency.value and a detune.value of 100 cents, making the note value C#3.

```
let audioContext = new AudioContext();
let oscillator = audioContext.createOscillator();
oscillator.connect(audioContext.destination);
oscillator.frequency.value = 130.81; //_____C3
oscillator.start(audioContext.currentTime);
oscillator.stop(audioContext.currentTime + 2);
oscillator.onended = function() {
  oscillator = audioContext.createOscillator();
  oscillator.frequency.value = 130.81; // C3 note
  oscillator.detune.value = 100; /*sets the note to one half step
    higher to C#3*/
  oscillator.connect(audioContext.destination);
  oscillator.start(audioContext.currentTime + 0.5);
  oscillator.stop(audioContext.currentTime + 2.5);
};
```

▮ Summary

In this chapter, you learned the basics of node graphs and oscillators. In the next chapter, you will learn the basics of HTML and CSS and create the interface for your first Web Audio API applications.

Using HTML and CSS to Build User Interfaces

In this chapter, you will learn the basics of HTML and CSS, giving you the necessary tools to build user interfaces for your Web Audio API applications. You will do this by building a user interface intended to trigger an oscillator that includes interactive controls to select frequency and waveform type. In the next chapter, you will combine the interface with JavaScript code to build your first working interactive application.

▋ What Is a User Interface?

A user interface, also called a *UI*, is the part of an application that a user interacts with. A music synthesizer's UI is the keyboard, as well as the knobs and sliders that allow you to modify the sound of the instrument. In a website or application, the UI can include buttons, form fields, sliders, scroll bars, and other elements that facilitate user control.

▋ HTML

HTML stands for *hypertext markup language* and is the language used to create static websites. In Chapter 1, you learned that HTML consists of elements, sometimes referred to as *tags*, that make up the page of an HTML document. To be treated as an HTML document, a file must be saved with .html appended to its name. A file extension is a group of characters placed after a period in a file name that indicates the file's format. In the case of a file named index.html, the file extension is .html.

The following code is from the HTML template you created in Chapter 1. It consists of a collection of elements required to make a document W3C compliant. W3C stands for *World Wide Web Consortium*; this group is responsible for the development of web standards. Unlike JavaScript, HTML does *not* return errors if your code is written incorrectly, so you need additional tools to find HTML errors. You can test the compliance of an HTML document by running your code through the HTML validation tool at the following URL: https://validator.w3.org.

```
<!DOCTYPE html>
<html>
  <head>
    <meta charset="UTF-8">
    <title>app</title>
    <script src="js/app.js"></script>
    <link rel="stylesheet" href="css/app.css">
  </head>
  <!--_____ BEGIN APP-->

  </body>
  <!--_____ END APP-->
</html>
```

▌ Explanation of the HTML Template

The first element in an HTML file, <!DOCTYPE>, declares what version of HTML the page is written in. For HTML5, use <!DOCTYPE html>. As of this writing, HTML5 is the newest version of the HTML specification. The next element, <html>, encapsulates the remainder of the code. <html> represents the "root" of the document and contains the <head> and elements. The <head> element describes information about the document, whereas the element describes the content on the visible page.

Within the <head> element, the <meta> tag defines which keyboard character encoding is used on the web page. Character encodings represent the way that characters on your physical keyboard get translated into text. UTF-8 covers most languages and is also the standard for the modern web. The <title> element is used to give your page a title. The remaining code inside the <head> element includes references to external files that contain JavaScript and CSS code.

Immediately before the body element is a comment. HTML comments are written using the following syntax:

```
<!--comment goes here -->
```

Inside the <body> element is where you write the bulk of your HTML code. In the following example, the <p> and <h1> elements between the opening and closing body tags show how HTML is used to display text. The <h1> element is a heading element and the <p> element is a paragraph element. As the names imply, you use the heading element to create title headings and the paragraph element to encapsulate text that represents a paragraph.

```html
<!DOCTYPE html>
<html>
  <head>
    <meta charset="UTF-8">
    <title>Template</title>
    <script src="js/app.js"></script>
    <link rel="stylesheet" href="css/app.css">
  </head>
  <!                                              BEGIN APP-->

    Creating an Interface </h1>
    In this chapter we will go over HTML and CSS</p>
  </body>
  <!--                                            END APP-->
</html>
```

▐ Understanding HTML Elements

In the HTML specification, there are over 100 elements to choose from. Each one of these has a specific use case. A full list is available at the following URL: https://developer.mozilla.org/en-US/docs/Web/HTML/Element.

The sheer number of elements may be daunting at first, but once you understand how to use a small handful of these elements, it becomes easier to learn the others. For the purposes of this chapter, only the following elements are used:

<div>	**Div element**
	Defines a general-purpose block-level container
<span>	**Span element**
	Defines a general-purpose inline container
<h1> to <h6>	**Heading element**
	Creates a heading title
<p>	**Paragraph element**
	Wraps paragraph text
<form>	**Form element**
	Encapsulates input elements and denotes form fields
<input>	**Input element**
	Creates entry fields for forms
<hr>	**Horizontal rule element**
	Displays a horizontal line
<ul>	**Unordered list element**
	Contains list elements
<li>	**List item element**
	Contains text that is an item in a list

When you write HTML and CSS, you must understand two primary concepts. First, HTML web pages consist of a hierarchy of elements that form a nested tree-like structure. This is called the *HTML Document Object Model* (or *DOM* for short). The following diagram reflects the node tree of the previous example.

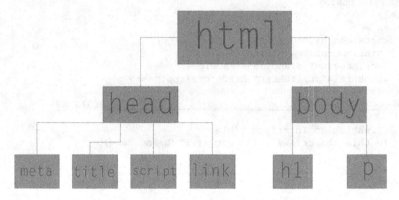

Second, most elements contain opening and closing tags that are used to encapsulate other elements. The processes of encapsulating elements within other elements and treating the containing elements as boxes are commonly referred to as the *box model*.

The following code emphasizes the box model by adding elements that contain other elements. This includes a containing <div> that encapsulates a <form> element. The <form> element then encapsulates <input>, <span>, and (paragraph) elements.

```
  Creating an Interface </h1>
  In this chapter we will go over HTML and CSS</p>
  <div>
    <form>
      <input id ="on-off" type = "button" value="start">
        <span>Click to start oscillator</span>
        Use slider to modify frequency</p>
      <input type= "range">
    </form>
  </div>
</body>
```

The tree structure of the modified HTML is reflected in the following diagram.

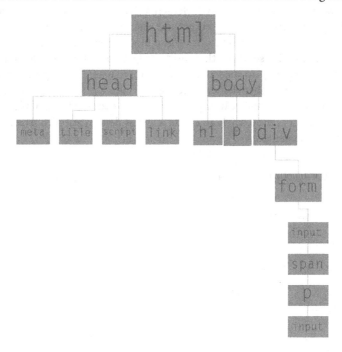

The rendering of the code looks like the following figure.

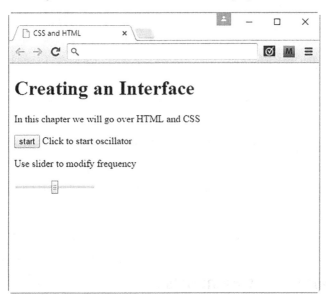

HTML elements come in two categories: *block-level* and *inline*. The difference between the two is that block-level elements display vertically and inline elements display horizontally. The <div> and <span> elements are two elements that reflect these characteristics. <div> is a block-level element and <span> is an inline element. These are both considered generic container elements. This means that they convey no special meaning but are useful to help lend structure to your page when no other elements are appropriate. The following code demonstrates how these elements are interpreted when they are rendered in the browser. The <hr> element is used solely to create a visual demarcation (horizontal line) between the two examples.

```
<span>
This text is inside a span
</span>
<span>
This text is inside a span
</span>
<hr>
<div>
This text is inside a div
</div>
<div>
This text is inside a div
</div>
</body>
```

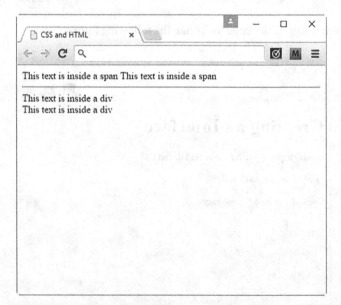

▌ Form and Input Elements

<form> is a block-level element intended to encapsulate <input> elements. <input> elements are used to create text fields, buttons, and range sliders. The type attribute is used to define the type of data the element is expected to

display, which can change how the element appears on the page. So for example, if you set the `type` attribute to `range`, it creates a slider.

```
<form>
  <input type = "range">
</form>
```

The `type` attribute comes with a built-in list of possible settings, some of which are shown in the following code. The `value` attribute gives the `<input>` element a default setting, as shown in the following demonstration code (code that is not used in your final application):

```
<form>
    Input element type set to "button"</p>
    <input type = "button" value="start">
    <hr>
    Input element type set to "range"</p>
    <input type= "range">
    <hr>
    Input element set to a "number"</p>
    <input type = "number" value="44.100">
    <hr>
    Input element set to a "text"</p>
    <input type= "text" value ="sine">
  </form>
</body>
```

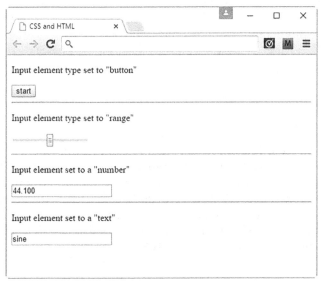

▐ CSS

CSS stands for *cascading style sheets* and is the technology used to style web pages and web applications. Like HTML, CSS does not throw errors when written improperly. To check for errors, you can use the W3C CSS validator tool at this URL: https://jigsaw.w3.org/css-validator/.

CSS files use the `.css` file extension. To use CSS with an HTML file, you must first create a CSS document and then connect it to your HTML document using the `<link>` element in the `<head>`. The following example illustrates this usage, which is applied for the remainder of this chapter.

```
<!DOCTYPE html>
<html>
  <head>
    <meta charset="UTF-8">
    <title>CSS and HTML</title>
    <link rel="stylesheet" href="css/app.css">
  </head>

    Creating an Interface </h1>
    In this chapter we will go over HTML and CSS</p>
    <div>
      <form>
        <input id ="on-off" type = "button" value="start">
        <span>Click to start oscillator</span>
        Use slider to modify frequency</p>
        <input type= "range">
      </form>
    </div>
  </body>
<html>
```

To ensure that your CSS document is being read properly, open your HTML document in Chrome and open the developer tools. If you made an error, the console will indicate this in red.

After the CSS file is linked you can begin to apply CSS styling to the HTML elements. For example, if you want to change the background color of the page, in your CSS file you select the body element and set the `background-color` property to a color value. This is shown in the following example where the background color is changed to orange. As an alternative to using the name of the color, you can set the color using a hex color code value such as `#ffa500` or a red–green–blue value such as `rgb(255,165,0)`.

```
body{
  background-color:orange;
}
```

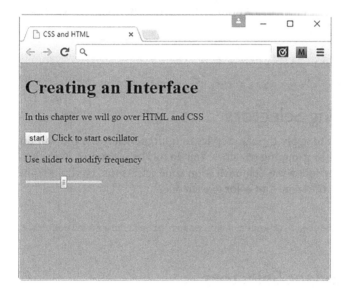

The procedure for applying CSS to an element is as follows:

1. Select the element you want to affect and type its name in your CSS file. In the previous example, this was body.

2. Type an opening and closing curly brace. These two braces are commonly referred to as a *code block*. Inside the code block, you place properties and set values following a colon. In the previous example, the property was background-color and its value was orange. Each property value setting ends with a semicolon.

The CSS specification includes many properties. A full list of properties is available at this URL: https://developer.mozilla.org/en-US/docs/Web/CSS/Reference.

▐█ Comments

Just like HTML or JavaScript, you can add comments to your CSS file using the following syntax:

```
/* This is a CSS comment */
```

▐█ Element Selectors

When you select elements directly, *all* instances of the element are selected and the same CSS styling is applied to them. For example, in the following demonstration code, every <div> on the page is selected and given a background color of blue.

```
div{
  background-color:blue;
}
```

▐█ Grouping Selectors

If you want to apply the same styles to multiple selectors, you can do so in one line of code by grouping selectors. You do this by separating each element with a comma. The following demonstration code selects the, p, <li>, and h1 elements and applies the same font color to each one.

```
p,li,h1{
  color:green; //Changes font color of all three elements to green
}
```

▐█ Descendent Selectors

If you want to access an element *only* if it is nested inside of a particular element, you can do this with descendent selectors. The CSS syntax for this type of selector is expressed by typing the parent element, a space, and then the element you want to select. In the following code, a descendant selector is used to select all <li> elements that are nested in any <div> element. In the following demonstration code, the font color of each <li> element is set to blue.

```
div li{
  color:blue;
}
```

It is important to realize that descendant selectors select all the descendent elements no matter how nested they are. If the previous CSS example were applied to the following HTML code, it would change the font color of all of the <li> elements to blue even though they are nested in a <ul> element.

```
<div>
  <ul>
    <li>Item-1</li>
    <li>Item-2</li>
    <li>Item-3</li>
  </ul>
</div>
```

▌ Child Selectors

Child selectors are similar to descendent selectors with the difference that the selected element can only be *one* level deep relative to the parent. A child selector is made using the ">" symbol with the parent element on its left side and the child element on its right. The following demonstration code will select all <li> elements that are children of <ul> elements.

```
ul > li{
  /* do something */
}
```

▌ class and id

Often when selecting elements, you do not want to select every element of a particular type. Rather, you might want to select either individual instances of elements or groups of elements. You can *single out* an individual element for styling by using an identifier called id. Conversely, you can designate a collection of elements as a *group* by using an identifier called class.

To single out an element using an id, you must first define id as an attribute of an HTML element. The syntax looks like the following:

```
<div id = "controls">
<!-- content -->
</div>
```

In your CSS, you can then select this individual element by preceding its id with a hashtag character.

```
#controls{
  /* properties and values go here */
}
```

Keep in mind that id names are intended to be used only once in your HTML and are applied to a *single* element!

▌ Modifying the App Interface

In the following code, an additional <div> is added to the page and encloses a collection of elements. You might be wondering why <h2> is used as the first element instead of another <h1>. The reason is that the number value of the heading element is intended to represent the precedence of the information contained

---

within it. The lowest number is most important and each higher number is less important. So for example, the information contained in the <h1> element should take precedence because it conveys more overall meaning as it relates to the web page. You might notice that there is a size difference in the way the browser renders these elements. You should ignore this size difference and focus on content precedence. You can always change the font size using CSS to make these elements any size you want, including setting them all to the same size.

The next element is <ul> with an id of oscillator-list. This element contains a series of <li> elements, each given an id name of a particular waveform type. <ul> is an *unordered list* element and is intended to encapsulate the <li> elements, which are *list* elements. As the name implies, these elements are used to create lists.

```
  Creating an Interface </h1>
 In this chapter we will go over HTML and CSS</p>
   <div>
     <form>
       <input id ="on-off" type = "button" value="start">
       <span>Click to start oscillator</span>
       Use slider to modify frequency</p>
       <input type= "range">
     </form>
   </div>
   <div>
     <h2>Waveform</h2>
     <ul id="oscillator-list">
       <li id="sawtooth">sawtooth</li>
       <li id="sine"> sine</li>
       <li id="triangle">triangle</li>
       <li id="square">square</li>
     </ul>
   </div>
</body>
```

In the following CSS, each `<li>` element is selected via its `id` and given a background color.

```css
#sawtooth{
  background-color: #336E91;
}
#sine{
  background-color: #783d47;
}
#triangle{
  background-color: #3b3040;
}
#square{
  background-color: #b85635;
}
```

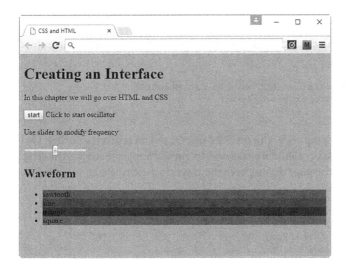

Now that you know how to single out an element using `id` selectors, it is time to learn how to group elements using class selectors.

In your HTML document, assign the two `<div>` elements the class osc-controls. Then encapsulate the first and inside a new `<div>`, and place another `<div>` element at the bottom of the page that contains a paragraph element with the phrase "JavaScript for Sound Artists Demo" inside of it.

You should have a total of four `<div>` elements in this code, which looks like this:

```html
<body>
  <div>
      Creating an Interface </h1>
      In this chapter we will go over HTML and CSS</p>
  </div>
  <div class="osc-controls">
    <form>
      <input id ="on-off" type = "button" value="start">
```

```
      <span>Click to start oscillator</span>
      Use slider to modify frequency</p>
      <input type= "range">
    </form>
  </div>
  <div class="osc-controls">
    <h2>Waveform</h2>
    <ul id="oscillator-list">
      <li id="sawtooth">sawtooth</li>
      <li id="sine"> sine</li>
      <li id="triangle">triangle</li>
      <li id="square">square</li>
    </ul>
  </div>
  <div>
    JavaScript for Sound Artists Demo</p>
  </div>
</body>
```

To select the osc-controls class from CSS, you must preface the class name with a dot.

```
.osc-controls{ /* Notice the dot selector */
  /* set property values */
}
```

In the following code, the osc-controls class is given a border. Only the middle two <div> elements respond to these changes because the first and third <div> on the page do not have the class osc-controls assigned to them.

```
.osc-controls {
  border-style:solid;
  border-color: #BC6527;
  border-width: 2px;
  border-radius:10px;
}
```

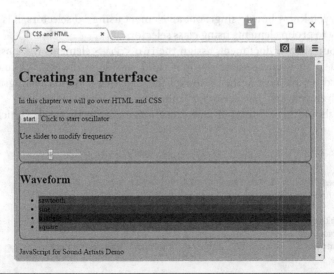

You might notice that the page looks a little awkward because the start button is now pushed up against the left edge of its container. Also, the two <divs> with borders are stacked directly on top of one another with no space between them. You could make this look a bit cleaner by creating some space between these elements. To do this, you should have an understanding of the following three properties: margin, border, and padding.

▌ Margin, Border, and Padding

Both block-level and inline elements have access to border, margin, and padding properties, although they respond to them differently. These three properties correspond to three layers of space around an element. The border property creates a border around an element. The padding property creates a layer of space that resides inside the border. The margin property creates a layer of space that resides outside the border.

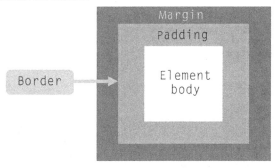

To create a bit of space between the text and a <div> element border, include the following code in your CSS file:

```
div{
    padding:20px;
}
```

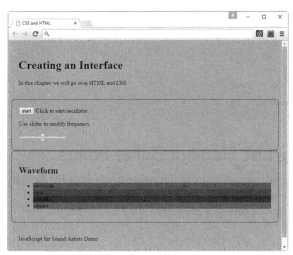

If you want to apply padding or a margin to only specific sides of an element, you can do so by using the following properties:

```
margin-top
margin-right
margin-bottom
margin-left
padding-top
padding-right
padding-bottom
padding-left
```

The two outlines around the middle <div> elements could use some space between them. The following code creates this space by using the bottom-margin property with a value of 20px.

```
.osc-controls {
  border-style:solid;
  border-color: #BC6527;
  border-width: 2px;
  border-radius:10px;
  margin-bottom:20px;
}
```

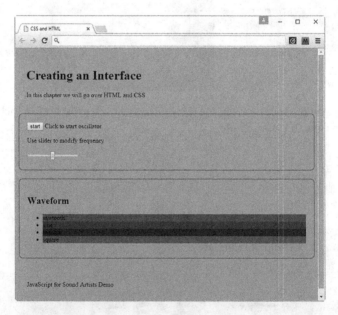

I Removing List Element Bullet Points

The following code removes the bullet points from each list item by selecting all of the <li> elements that are descendants of an element with an id of oscillator-list and applying a property called list-style-type with a value of none.

```
#oscillator-list li{ /* Descendent selector */
  list-style-type: none;
}
```

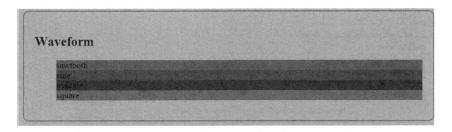

You can remove the space previously occupied by the bullet points by setting the padding-left property to zero on the parent <ul> element.

```
#oscillator-list{
  padding-left:0px;
}
```

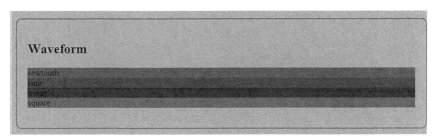

▓ Font Size, Style (Type), and Color

As a touch-up, the following code selects all the elements that harbor text and sets their font size to 1.5em, which is a bit larger than the current value. An em is equivalent to a parent element's font size, or, if there is no parent, the web browser's default text size. For most web browsers, this value is about 16 pixels, which in CSS is written as 16px. Therefore, assuming there is no parent element, 2em is equivalent to 32 pixels and 1.5em to 24 pixels.

```
p,span,li,input{
  font-size:1.5em;
}
```

The default font type for Chrome is Times New Roman. You can change the font type if you like. The following code changes the font type to Arial.

```
body{
  background-color:orange;
  font-family: "Arial";
}
```

The font color of the text describing the waveform types is black, which is difficult to read because the background color of each <li> is dark. The following code changes the text color property to white.

```
#oscillator-list li{
  list-style-type: none;
  color:white;
}
```

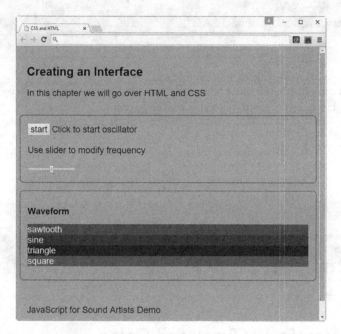

█ Centering Block-Level Elements

If you want to center a block-level element, you can do so by setting its width to a value smaller than its containing element and applying a margin property with a value of 0 auto. This sets the left and right margin values to automatically extend to the boundaries of the container, centering the element. In the following code, a <div> with a class of application contains all the HTML within the body element. Its CSS is set to a fixed width and centered by specifying margin: 0 auto.

```
<div class="application">
  <div>
     Creating an Interface </h1>
    In this chapter we will go over HTML and CSS</p>
  </div>
  <div class="osc-controls">
    <form>
      <input id ="on-off" type = "button" value="start">
      <span>Click to start oscillator</span>
```

```
          Use slider to modify frequency</p>
          <input type= "range">
        </form>
      </div>
      <div class="osc-controls">
        <h2>Waveform</h2>
        <ul id="oscillator-list">
          <li id="sawtooth">sawtooth</li>
          <li id="sine"> sine</li>
          <li id="triangle">triangle</li>
          <li id="square">square</li>
        </ul>
      </div>
      <div>
        JavaScript for Sound Artists Demos</p>
      </div>
    </div>
  </div>
</body>
```

The CSS for the newly created div is as follows.

```
.application{
  width:550px;
  margin:0 auto;
}
```

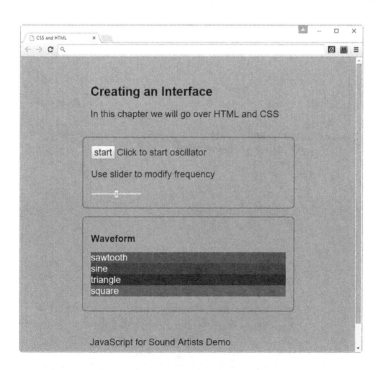

As a final step, remove the first element and replace the text of the element with the title *Oscillator Generator*. The final HTML code for the application is below.

```
<div class="application">
  <div>
     Oscillator Generator </h1>
  </div>
  <div class="osc-controls">
    <form>
      <input id ="on-off" type = "button" value="start">
      <span>Click to start oscillator</span>
      Use slider to modify frequency</p>
      <input type= "range">
    </form>
  </div>
  <div class="osc-controls">
    <h2>Waveform</h2>
    <ul id="oscillator-list">
      <li id="sawtooth">sawtooth</li>
      <li id="sine"> sine</li>
      <li id="triangle">triangle</li>
      <li id="square">square</li>
    </ul>
  </div>
  <div>
    JavaScript for Sound Artists Demo</p>
  </div>
</div>
```

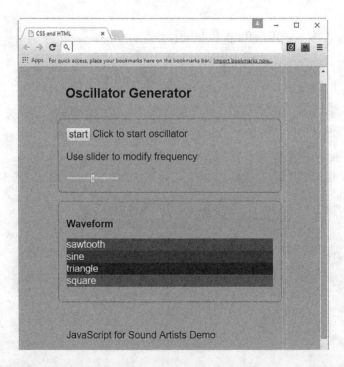

The final CSS code for the application is as follows.

```css
body {
  background-color: orange;
  font-family: "Arial";
}

.application {
  width: 550px;
  margin: 0 auto;
}

p,
span,
li,
input {
  font-size: 1.5em;
}


#sawtooth {
  background-color: #336E91;
}

#sine {
  background-color: #783d47;
}

#triangle {
  background-color: #3b3040;
}

#square {
  background-color: #b85635;
}

 .osc-controls {
  border-style: solid;
  border-color: #BC6527;
  border-width: 2px;
  border-radius: 10px;
  margin-bottom: 20px;
}

div {
  padding: 20px;
}

#oscillator-list li {
  /* Descendent selector */
  list-style-type: none;
  color: white;
}

#oscillator-list {
  padding-left: 0px;
}
```

▌ Summary

In this chapter, you created the user interface for a small application. In the next chapter, you will add JavaScript code to make the application fully functional.

9 DOM Programming with JavaScript

This chapter shows you how to add JavaScript to CSS and HTML. By the end of the chapter, you will have created a fully functioning application with interactive controls.

▮ How Does JavaScript Communicate with the DOM?

The DOM (Document Object Model) contains a collection of JavaScript properties and methods that allows you to manipulate HTML elements and to write code that responds to user-invoked actions such as mouse clicks and form submissions. Typically, when writing an application, you want to ask yourself two things. The first is, *what do you want or expect the user to do*? The second is, *what should happen in response to user actions*? So for example, the following code contains a play button, and when a user clicks it the browser runs a built-in function called alert. This function displays a pop-up with the message: You clicked play.

▮ HTML

```
<body>
  <input id="play-button" type="button" value="PLAY">
</body>
```

DOI: 10.1201/9781003201496-9

▮ JavaScript

```javascript
window.onload = function() {
  let playButton = document.getElementById("play-button");
  playButton.addEventListener("click", function() {
    alert("You clicked the play button");
  });
};
```

The first line of JavaScript, `window.onload = function(){}`, restricts the code in the function scope from running until all of the HTML code has loaded. If the JavaScript were to load before the HTML, then any JavaScript intended to affect HTML elements or respond to user events like mouse clicks would either not be recognized or would be only partially recognized. The result in either of these cases is nonworking code.

The next line selects a DOM element with an `id` of `play-button` and stores it in a variable called `playButton`. This is done using `getElement-ById`, a method of the `document` object.

The `document` object is not part of the core JavaScript language. Instead, it is an object provided by the DOM API, making it part of the web browser.

```javascript
let playButton = document.getElementById("play-button");
```

The next line of code applies the `eventListener` method to the `playButton`.

```javascript
playButton.addEventListener("click", function() {
  alert("You clicked the play button");
});
```

The `playButton.addEventListener` method waits for a user to apply an action and then invokes a callback function. In this case, the action is a mouse click and is specified in the first argument of the function. The second argument is the callback. The callback runs when the user clicks on the element with the `id` of `play-button`, which invokes `alert()`.

The JavaScript DOM API contains many methods and properties. In this chapter, only the following of these are used.

Method or Property	Description
addEventListener	Allows elements to respond to user events such as mouse clicks
getElementById	Selects an element by id
getElementsByTagName	Selects elements by tag name
getElementsByClassName	Selects elements by class
classList.add	Adds a class to an element
classList.contains	Checks whether an element has a specified class name
classList.remove	Removes a class from an element
setAttribute	Sets an attribute on an element
innerHTML	Gets and sets the content of an element
value	Sets or gets the value of an input element

Building the Application

In the previous chapter, you built a user interface using CSS and HTML. You are now going to write the code to make this a working JavaScript application. To get started, create a copy of the final project in Chapter 8 and make sure you create a folder that contains a file named app.js. Your directory structure should look like the one in the following image.

In the app.js file, make sure you have strict mode enabled. All JavaScript code is written below the use strict string.

```
"use strict";
```

Set your index.html file to reference the app.js file.

```
<head>
  <meta charset="UTF-8">
  <title>CSS and HTML</title>
  <script src="js/app.js"></script>
  <link rel="stylesheet" href="css/app.css">
</head>
```

How to Trigger an Oscillator by Clicking a Button

The user interface you created in the previous chapter contained a button with the id of on-off. You are now going to write code to start an oscillator playing when this button is clicked.

```
"use strict";
const   audioContext = new AudioContext();
window.onload = function() {
  let   onOff = document.getElementById("on-off");
  onOff.addEventListener("click", function() {
    let osc = audioContext.createOscillator();
    osc.type = "sawtooth";
```

```
      osc.frequency.value = 300;
      osc.connect(audioContext.destination);
      osc.start(audioContext.currentTime);
   });
};
```

Although this code starts the oscillator playing, it does not *stop* it from play-ing. The following changes implement the stop feature by adding a conditional statement to addEventListener to check whether a variable named osc is set to false. If osc is false, an oscillator is created and assigned to it. This makes the Boolean value of the osc variable true, and the start method is invoked, allowing the oscillator to play. If the user clicks the **Start** button again, the condi-tional statement sees that the osc variable has the Boolean value true and runs the code in the else branch. This stops the oscillator from playing and resets osc to false.

```
"use strict";
const audioContext = new AudioContext();
window.onload = function() {
  let onOff = document.getElementById("on-off");
  /*_____BEGIN set initial
    osc state to false*/
  let osc = false;
  /*_____END set initial
    osc state to false*/
  onOff.addEventListener("click", function() {
    /*_____BEGIN Conditional
      statement to check if osc is TRUE or FALSE*/
    if (!osc) { /*_____Is osc false? If so then
      create and assign oscillator to osc and play it.*/
      osc = audioContext.createOscillator();
      osc.type = "sawtooth";
      osc.frequency.value = 300;
      osc.connect(audioContext.destination);
      osc.start(audioContext.currentTime);
      /*_____Otherwise stop it and
        reset osc to false for next time.*/
    } else {
      osc.stop(audioContext.currentTime);
      osc = false;
    }
    /*_____END Conditional
      statement to check if osc is TRUE or FALSE*/
  });
};
```

▮ Toggling the *Start/Stop* Text

Though the code in the previous example works, the following feature makes it more user-friendly: Program the button text and associated span element text to display the words *start* or *stop* depending on whether the oscillator is playing or not.

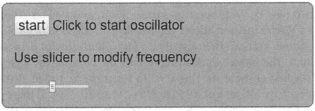

You can implement this feature as follows:

```
"use strict";
const  audioContext = new AudioContext();
window.onload = function() {
  let  onOff = document.getElementById("on-off");
  let span = document.getElementsByTagName("span")[0];
  /*_____BEGIN set initial osc
     state to false*/
  let  osc = false;
  /*_____END set initial osc
     state to false*/
  onOff.addEventListener("click", function() {
    /*_____BEGIN Conditional
       statement to check if osc is TRUE or FALSE*/
    if (!osc) { /*_____Is osc false? If so then
         create and assign oscillator to osc variable and play it.*/
      osc = audioContext.createOscillator();
      osc.type = "sawtooth";
      osc.frequency.value = 300;
      osc.connect(audioContext.destination);
      osc.start(audioContext.currentTime);
      onOff.value = "stop";
      span.innerHTML = "Click to stop oscillator";
      /*_____Otherwise stop it and
         reset osc to false for next time.*/
    } else {
      osc.stop(audioContext.currentTime);
      osc = false;
      onOff.value = "start";
      span.innerHTML = "Click to start oscillator";
    }
    /*_____END Conditional
       statement to check if osc is TRUE or FALSE*/
  });
};
```

This code introduces a new DOM method called getElementsByTagName as well as two new DOM properties: innerHTML and value. The getElementsByTagName method allows you to select a collection of elements on the page by tag name. You can then specify an *individual* element using array-style index selectors. The index selection represents the order of the element on the page, with the first element starting at 0. To select the first span element on the page, you specify getElementsByTagName("span")[0]. If there are several span elements and you want to select the third one from the top of the page, you specify the index as 2, and the selector looks like this:

```
document.getElementsByTagName("span")[2]
```

It is important to understand that DOM elements are *not* arrays, even though the notation used to select them is similar to that used for arrays. DOM elements are referred to as *nodes*.

▌ Programming the Frequency Slider

You are now going to add functionality to the frequency slider. The following code shows how you capture the value of the frequency slider when the oscillator is clicked. This is done using the value property. The value is then stored in a variable named freqSliderVal and represents the frequency of the oscillator. Additionally, the freqSliderVal is logged to the console, allowing you to see changes made to it.

```
"use strict";
const audioContext = new AudioContext();
window.onload = function() {
  let onOff = document.getElementById("on-off");
  let  span = document.getElementsByTagName("span")[0];
  /*_____BEGIN set initial osc
    state to false*/
  let osc = false;
  /*_____END set initial osc
    state to false*/
  onOff.addEventListener("click", function() {
    /*_____BEGIN Conditional
      statement to check if osc is TRUE or FALSE*/
    let  freqSliderVal = document.getElementsByTagName(" input")
[1].
    value;
    console.log(freqSliderVal);
    if (!osc) { /*_____Is osc false? If so then
        create and assign oscillator to osc variable and play it.*/
      osc = audioContext.createOscillator();
      osc.type = "sawtooth";
      osc.frequency.value = freqSliderVal;
      osc.connect(audioContext.destination);
      osc.start(audioContext.currentTime);
      onOff.value = "stop";
      span.innerHTML = "Click to stop oscillator";
      /*_____Otherwise stop it and
```

```
            reset osc to false for next time.*/
        } else {
            osc.stop(audioContext.currentTime);
            osc = false;
            onOff.value = "start";
            span.innerHTML = "Click to start oscillator";
        }
        /*_____END Conditional
        statement to check if osc is TRUE or FALSE*/
    });
};
```

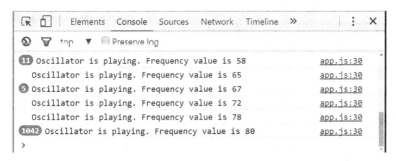

Changing the Frequency in Real Time

The code in the previous example works, but there is a cost. To hear the frequency changes, the user must turn the oscillator off, move the frequency slider, and then start the oscillator again. You could provide a seamless experience if the user could hear the effect in real time while moving the slider. To implement this, you can use setInterval() to check for state changes of the range slider and then apply them to the osc.frequency value.

The purpose of setInterval() is to invoke a function repeatedly at a specified time interval. In the following code, setInterval() takes two arguments. The first is a callback and the second is a number that represents a millisecond interval value (in this case, 50 ms). When setInterval() runs, the callback is invoked repeatedly at the time interval specified in the second argument. The freqSliderVal variable has been placed outside the scope of both the onOff.addEventListener and setInterval methods so that both of them have access to it. The setInterval method contains a conditional statement that checks to see whether osc is false, and if so displays the message "Oscillator is stopped. Waiting for oscillator to start", in the console. The moment the oscillator starts, setInterval() reassigns freqSliderVal to the respective <input> range value and assigns that value to osc.frequency. value. Because setInterval() does this in 50-ms increments, it creates near real-time change in the oscillator frequency when you move the frequency slider.

```
"use strict";
const audioContext = new AudioContext();
window.onload = function() {
    let   onOff = document.getElementById("on-off");
```

```
let span = document.getElementsByTagName("span")[0];
/*_____BEGIN set initial osc
   state to false*/
let  osc = false;
/*_____END set initial osc
   state to false*/
/*_____BEGIN set initial
   frequency value*/
let freqSliderVal = document.getElementsByTagName("input")[1].
   value;
/*_____END set initial
   frequency value*/
/*_____BEGIN check range
   slider value and set frequency of oscillator*/
setInterval(function() {
   if (!osc) {
      console.log("Oscillator is stopped. Waiting for oscillator to
         start");
   } else {
      freqSliderVal = document.getElementsByTagName("input")[1].
value;
      osc.frequency.value = freqSliderVal;
      console.log("Oscillator is playing. Frequency value is " +
         freqSliderVal);
   }
}, 50);
/*_____End check range slider
   value and set frequency of oscillator*/
onOff.addEventListener("click", function() {
   /*_____BEGIN Conditional
      statement to check if osc is TRUE or FALSE*/
   if (!osc) { /*_____Is osc false? If so then
         create and assign oscillator to osc variable and play it.*/
      osc = audioContext.createOscillator();
      osc.type = "sawtooth";
      osc.frequency.value = freqSliderVal;
      osc.connect(audioContext.destination);
      osc.start(audioContext.currentTime);
      onOff.value = "stop";
      span.innerHTML = "Click to stop oscillator";
      /*_____Otherwise stop it and
         reset osc to false for next time.*/
   } else {
      osc.stop(audioContext.currentTime);
      osc = false;
      onOff.value = "start";
      span.innerHTML = "Click to start oscillator";
   }
   /*_____END Conditional
      statement to check if osc is TRUE or FALSE*/
});
};
```

■ Changing Waveform Types

You are now going to write code to allow users to click one of the four waveforms on the page and set the oscillator to play the selected waveform.

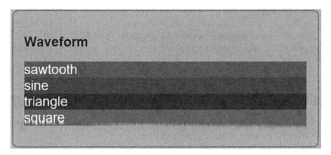

To do this, use the eventListener() method to capture the id of the element clicked by the user. Because the id of each <li> is the name of a waveform, you must assign this id to the osc.type property. You want users to be able to update the waveform type without having to repeatedly restart the oscillator, and you can do this similarly to the frequency slider changes in the previous example.

In the following code, you create a variable named selectedWaveform to give the oscillator a default waveform type and to store any selected waveform changes.

```
let selectedWaveform = "sawtooth";
```

This value is then assigned to osc.type.

```
if (!osc) {
  osc = audioContext.createOscillator();
  osc.type = selectedWaveform;
  osc.frequency.value = freqSliderVal;
  osc.connect(audioContext.destination);
  osc.start(audioContext.currentTime);
  onOff.value = "stop";
  span.innerHTML = "Click to stop oscillator";
}
```

Next, create a variable named waveformTypes and assign it the result of calling getElementsByTagName(). The waveformTypes value is used to select one of the four <li> elements on the page.

```
let waveformTypes = document.getElementsByTagName('li');
```

Next, create a function named select that is used as a callback for a series of event listeners used to select the id of the <li> clicked by the user.

```
function select() {
  selectedWaveform = document.getElementById(this.id).id;
  console.log(selectedWaveform); // Outputs id
}
```

Next, a for loop is used to examine each <li> node and assign an event listener to each one. Each event listener is set to respond to a click event that invokes the callback function select. When the select function runs, it captures the id of the <li> element clicked by the user. This id is then stored in the selectedWaveform variable.

```
for (let  i = 0; i < waveformTypes.length; i++) {
  waveformTypes[i].addEventListener('click', select, false);
}
```

▮ Completed Code with Waveform Selection

```
"use strict";
let audioContext = new AudioContext();
window.onload = function() {
  let onOff = document.getElementById("on-off");
  let span = document.getElementsByTagName("span")[0];
  let osc = false;
  let freqSliderVal = document.getElementsByTagName("input")[1].
value;
  /*_____BEGIN set selected
    waveform type value*/
  let selectedWaveform = "sawtooth";
  /*_____END set selected
    waveform type value*/
  /*_____BEGIN select all <li>
    elements*/
  let waveformTypes = document.getElementsByTagName('li');
  /*_____END select all <li>
    elements*/
  /*_____BEGIN callback to
    select <li> by id and assign id name to selectWaveform*/
  function select() {
    selectedWaveform = document.getElementById(this.id).id;
    console.log(selectedWaveform);
  }
  /*_____END callback to select
    <li> by id and assign id name to selectWaveform*/
  /*_____BEGIN loop through all
    <li> elements and set a click eventListener on them*/
  for (let i = 0; i < waveformTypes.length; i++) {
    waveformTypes[i].addEventListener('click', select);
  }
  /*_____END loop through all
    <li> elements and set a click eventListener on them*/
  setInterval(function() {
    if (!osc) {
      console.log("Oscillator is stopped. Waiting for oscillator to
        start");
    } else {
      freqSliderVal = document.getElementsByTagName("input")[1].
        value;
      osc.frequency.value = freqSliderVal;
      console.log("Oscillator is playing. Frequency value is " +
        freqSliderVal);
```

```
          osc.type = selectedWaveform;
      }
    }, 50);
    onOff.addEventListener("click", function() {
      if (!osc) {
        osc = audioContext.createOscillator();
        osc.type = selectedWaveform;
        osc.frequency.value = freqSliderVal;
        osc.connect(audioContext.destination);
        osc.start(audioContext.currentTime);
        onOff.value = "stop";
        span.innerHTML = "Click to stop oscillator";
      } else {
        osc.stop(audioContext.currentTime);
        osc = false;
        onOff.value = "start";
        span.innerHTML = "Click to start oscillator";
      }
    });
};
```

■ Giving an Outline to the Selected Waveform Type

When a user selects a waveform type, there is no visual cue that identifies the type selected. The following code adds a white outline to the selected waveform.

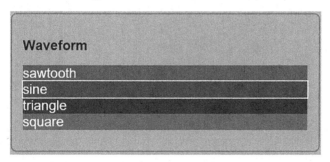

In the CSS file, create a class named selected-waveform and give it an outline property with a width of 2 pixels and the color white. Then, add this class dynamically to the <li> element that corresponds to the selected waveform type. To remove the selected waveform class of the previously selected element, use a for loop to examine all of the <li> elements and invoke classList.remove("selected-waveform") on each one.

In the CSS file, create the class.

```
.selected-waveform{
  outline:2px solid white;
}
```

In the JavaScript file, add the following code to the `select` function.

```
function select() {
  //_____BEGIN select element by id
  let  selectedWaveformElement = document.getElementById(this.id);
  //_____END select element by id
  selectedWaveform = document.getElementById(this.id).id;
  console.log(selectedWaveform);
  /*_____BEGIN remove any
    previously added selected-waveform classes*/
  for (let i = 0; i < waveformTypes.length; i += 1) {
    waveformTypes[i].classList.remove("selected-waveform");
  }
  /*_____END remove any previously
    added selected-waveform classes*/
  /*_____BEGIN add the selected-
    waveform class to the selected element*/
  selectedWaveformElement.classList.add("selected-waveform");
  /*_____END add the selected-
    waveform class to the selected element*/
}
```

▌ Summary

In this chapter, you learned how JavaScript interacts with the DOM. In the next chapter, you will learn the basics of a library named JQuery that makes DOM programming with **JavaScript** easier.

10 Simplifying DOM Programming with JQuery

In the previous chapter, you learned how JavaScript interacts with the DOM. In this chapter, you will learn how to simplify the process of adding interactive components to your application by using a library called *JQuery*. The objective of this chapter is not to teach you the entire JQuery API, but to give you the foundational knowledge to make JQuery a part of your programming toolkit. You can find the JQuery API at this URL: https://api.jquery.com/.

■ What is JQuery?

JQuery is a library written in JavaScript intended primarily for DOM manipulation. A library is a collection of preassembled code pieces designed to make a particular group of tasks easier. JQuery contains a large collection of methods and properties that can be used individually or combined to help ease the complexity of JavaScript DOM programming.

■ JQuery Setup

You can set up JQuery in one of two ways. The first is to download the library and reference it from an HTML file. The second is to reference it from a content delivery network (*CDN*). A CDN is a service accessible through the World Wide Web where you can reference code libraries and other files. The downside of using a CDN is that you will always need a working Internet connection to access it.

■ Referencing JQuery Directly

To reference JQuery directly, first download the library at this URL: http://jquery. com/. Next, use the following code as an example of how to reference the library. Your version of JQuery might be newer than 3.6.0.

```
<!DOCTYPE html>
<html>
  <head>
    <meta charset="UTF-8">
    <title></title>
    <script type="text/javascript" src="js/jquery- 3.6.0.min"
      charset="utf-8"></script>
    <script src="js/app.js"></script>
    <link rel="stylesheet" href="css/app.css">
  </head>
  <!--_____ BEGIN APP-->
  <body>
  </body>
  <!--_____ END APP-->
</html>
```

■ Using JQuery from a CDN

The following code references JQuery from a Google CDN library collection at this URL: https://developers.google.com/speed/libraries/.

```
<!DOCTYPE html>
<html>
  <head>
    <meta charset="UTF-8">
    <title></title>
    <script type="text/javascript" src="https://ajax.googleapis.
com/ajax/libs/jquery/3.6.0/jquery.min.js " charset="utf-8">
    </script>
    <script src="js/app.js"></script>
    <link rel="stylesheet" href="css/app.css">
  </head>
  <!--_____ BEGIN APP-->
  <body>
  </body>
  <!--_____ END APP-->
</html>
```

In the previous chapter, your JavaScript code was encapsulated in the following function:

```
window.onload = function() {
  // code goes here
};
```

This was done to ensure that the code loads *after* the browser renders the HTML document. JQuery comes bundled with a function that does the same thing with slightly different syntax.

```
$(function(){
  // code goes here
});
```

How to Use JQuery

The most fundamental use cases for JQuery require knowledge of two things. The first is how to *select* an HTML element. The second is how to *do something* with that element.

Selecting HTML Elements

The following code shows how to select an HTML element.

```
$("div") // this selects all div elements on the page
```

The syntax for element selectors always begins with a dollar sign, followed by two parentheses. You place the element wrapped in quotes inside the parentheses. JQuery selectors borrow from CSS selector syntax. If you know how to select elements using CSS, you can quickly learn to select elements in JQuery. The following are a few examples of CSS selectors and their JQuery counterparts:

Selection Type	CSS	JQuery
Element	div{}	$("div")
Child	p > span{}	$("p > span")
Descendent	p span{}	$("p span")
Multi	div, span, p{}	$("div, span, p ")
id	#item{}	$("#item")
Class	.item{}	$(".item")

Storing DOM Selectors as Variables

In some circumstances, you might find it aesthetically preferable to store your DOM selectors as variables. The following code is a modified version of the previous example with the div selector stored in a variable. The variable is preceded by a dollar sign to emphasize that it is a JQuery selector. Storing the DOM selector as a variable has the same effect as selecting the element directly.

```
$(function() {
  let $transportControl = $("div");
});
```

▮ Using Methods

After you have selected an element, you can modify it in some way using JQuery's built-in methods. JQuery comes with a large collection of methods; however, in this chapter, we are only going to use the following methods:

Method	Summary
on	Attaches event listeners to an element
css	Modifies the CSS of an element
fadeIn	Fades in an element over time
fadeOut	Fades out an element over time
val	Sets or gets the value attribute of an input element
addClass	Adds a class to an element
removeClass	Removes a class from an element
eq	Selects an element based on an index value
text	Sets or gets the text of an element

The following is an example of using css() to modify the look of an element. css() can be used either to change a single property or to set multiple properties using an object as an argument. An example of both use cases is given in the following code:

▮ HTML

```
<div>Play</div>
<div>Stop</div>
<div>Rewind</div>
<div>Fast Forward</div>
<div>Pause</div>
```

To change a single property:

JQuery/JavaScript to Change a Single Property

```
$(function() {
  $("div").css("background-color","orange");
});
```

To change multiple properties:

JQuery/JavaScript to Change Multiple Properties

```
$(function() {
  $("div").css({
    backgroundColor:"orange",
    width:"100px",
    borderStyle:"solid"
  });
});
```

Method Chaining

If you want to apply multiple methods to an element, you can connect them in succession so that they are invoked one after another. This is called *method chaining*.

In the following code, all of the div elements have their CSS display property set to none. JQuery is used to select the div elements and set their CSS properties using css(). The fadeIn method is then chained to each div, so that every div on the page fades in over the course of 1 second (1000 milliseconds). The first argument of fadeIn() is the duration of the animation in milliseconds. When fadeIn()completes, the fadeOut method is invoked, which fades out all div elements over the course of 1 second.

HTML

```
<div>Play</div>
<div>Stop</div>
<div>Rewind</div>
<div>Fast Forward</div>
<div>Pause</div>
```

CSS

```
div{
   display:none;
}
```

JQuery/JavaScript

```
$(function() {
  $("div").css({
    backgroundColor: "orange",
    width: "100px",
    borderStyle: "solid"
  }).fadeIn(1000).fadeOut(1000); // example of method chaining
});
```

The following HTML code contains an input element with its type attribute set to button. This is selected with JQuery and set to respond to click events *via* an event listener. The method used for this is on(), which takes two arguments. The first argument is a string that defines the event type and the second is a callback that is invoked when the event is fired.

HTML

```
<input type="button" value = "Play">
```

▌ JQuery/JavaScript

```
$(function() {
  $("input").on("click",function(){ //click event listener
    alert("You clicked play");
  });
});
```

▌ The this Keyword

The this keyword in JQuery can be used as a shorthand for the currently selected DOM element. The following HTML code contains three input elements. Using JQuery, these three elements are assigned a click event listener. When a user clicks an input button, the $(this) selector is used to single out the individual element the user clicked. The val method returns the value attribute of the clicked element.

▌ HTML

```
<input type="button" value = "Play">
<input type="button" value = "Pause">
<input type="button" value = "Stop">
```

▌ JQuery/JavaScript

```
$(function() {
  $("input").on("click",function(){ /*assign event listener to all
    input elements*/
  console.log($(this).val()); /*use the this keyword to access the
    element clicked and return its value property*/
  });
});
```

▌ Refactoring the Oscillator Player to Use JQuery

Now that you understand some JQuery basics, you are going to refactor the application you created in the previous chapter by replacing the built-in JavaScript DOM methods with JQuery selectors and methods.

Copy the completed code from the previous chapter to a new directory. In your index.html file reference the JQuery library.

```
<head>
  <meta charset="UTF-8">
  <title>CSS and HTML</title>
  <script type="text/javascript" src="
ttps://ajax.googleapis.com/ajax/libs/jquery/3.6.0/jquery.min.js
 charset="utf-8">
    </script>
  <script src="js/app.js"></script>
  <link rel="stylesheet" href="css/app.css">
</head>
```

Replace the app.js file with a new *empty* file with the same name.

In the old application, you used this function to encapsulate your code:

```
window.onload = function() {
}
```

In the new version of your code, make sure you replace window.onload with the equivalent JQuery function. Also put "use strict" and the AudioContext instantiation at the top of the file, as in the following example:

```
"use strict";
const audioContext = new AudioContext();
$(function(){
  // all code will go here
});
```

Next, modify the first three variables of the JavaScript file to use JQuery selectors.

Without JQuery

```
1  "use strict";
2  const audioContext = new AudioContext();
3  window.onload = function() {
4      let onOff = document.getElementById("on-off");
5      let span = document.getElementsByTagName("span")[0];
6      let osc = false;
7      let freqSliderVal = document.getElementsByTagName("input")[1].value;
8      let selectedWaveform = "sawtooth";
9  |
```

With JQuery

```
1  "use strict";
2  const audioContext = new AudioContext();
3  |
4  $(function() {
5      let $onOff = $("#on-off"); //                    JQuery selector
6      let $messageText = $("span"); //                 JQuery selector
7      let $freqSliderVal = $("input").eq(1).val(); //  JQuery selector
8      let osc = false;
9      let selectedWaveform = "sawtooth";
```

This code uses $("#on-off") to select the oscillator start or stop button by id. It is denoted by the hash selector. You then use $("span") to select the span that contains message text. This selection is done by element and, because there is only one span element on the page, you do not need to be more specific. Lastly, $("input").eq(1).val() is used to select the range slider value of the second input element on the page, which is stored in a variable named $freqSliderVal. This is done by making a general element selection for all input elements and specifying the second one on the page with the eq(1) method. The eq() method enables selection of elements by index with its argument being the index value. Once the correct input element is selected, val() is used to get its *value* attribute.

Setting Up the Event Listener for the User-Selected List Element

In the old application, the user interface code for oscillator selection was a bit complex. First, you needed to create a loop that attached a click event listener to all <li> elements. Then you created a function named select to be invoked as a callback for each of those event listeners. When the user clicked an <li> element, the select() callback looped through every <li> and removed any class identifiers titled selected-waveform. It then assigned the selected-waveform class to *only* the clicked element.

With JQuery, much of this complexity can be avoided. The following images show the contrast between the old version and a refined JQuery implementation.

Event Listener without JQuery

```
   app.js         ●
 1  "use strict";
 2  const audioContext = new AudioContext();
 3  window.onload = function() {
 4      let onOff = document.getElementById("on-off");
 5      let span = document.getElementsByTagName("span")[0];
 6      let osc = false;
 7      let freqSliderVal = document.getElementsByTagName("input")[1].value;
 8      let selectedWaveform = "sawtooth";
 9
10
11      //_____ BEGIN select all <li> elements
12      let waveformTypes = document.getElementsByTagName('li');
13
14      function select() {
15
16          let selectedWaveformElement = document.getElementById(this.id);
17          selectedWaveform = document.getElementById(this.id).id;
18  |
19
20          for (let i = 0; i < waveformTypes.length; i += 1) {
21              waveformTypes[i].classList.remove("selected-waveform");
22          }
23
24
25          selectedWaveformElement.classList.add("selected-waveform");
26
27      }
28
29      for (let i = 0; i < waveformTypes.length; i++) {
30          waveformTypes[i].addEventListener('click', select);
31      }
32
33      //_____ END select all <li> elements
34
```

Event Listener with JQuery

```
app.js
1   "use strict";
2   const audioContext = new AudioContext();
3
4   $(function() {
5       let $onOff = $("#on-off"); //_____ JQuery selector
6       let $messageText = $("span"); //_____ JQuery selector
7       let $freqSliderVal = $("input").eq(1).val(); //____ JQuery selector
8       let osc = false;
9       let selectedWaveform = "sawtooth";
10
11      //_____ BEGIN <li> selection code
12
13      $("li").on("click", function() {
14          selectedWaveform = this.id;
15          $("li").removeClass("selected-waveform");
16          $(this).addClass("selected-waveform");
17
18      });
19
20      //_____ END <li> selection code
21  |
```

The refactored JQuery code assigns a click event listener to all <li> elements.
When the user clicks an <li> element, its id is stored in a variable named
selectedWaveform. selectedWaveform is referenced in a higher scope
and is used later to set the oscillator type. The removeClass() method is used
to remove the selected-waveform class from *all* <li> elements. The last line
of code uses $(this) to select the *specific* <li> the user clicked and invokes
addClass() to give it the class selected-waveform.

Modifying the Code in setInterval

The only modification you need to make to setInterval is the replacement of
freqSliderVal with a JQuery DOM selector.

setInterval Method without JQuery

```
app.js
52  |
53      setInterval(function() {
54
55          if (!osc) {
56
57              console.log("Oscillator is stopped. Waiting for oscillator to start");
58
59          } else {
60
61              freqSliderVal = document.getElementsByTagName("input")[1].value;
62              osc.frequency.value = freqSliderVal;
63              console.log("Oscillator is playing. Frequency value is " + freqSliderVal);
64              osc.type = selectedWaveform;
65          }
66
67
68      }, 50);
69
```

setInterval Method with JQuery

```
app.js          x
22      setInterval(function() {
23          if (!osc) {
24              console.log("Oscillator is stopped. Waiting for oscillator to start");
25          } else {
26
27              $freqSliderVal = $("input").eq(1).val()
28              osc.frequency.value = $freqSliderVal;
29              console.log("Oscillator is playing. Frequency value is " + $freqSliderVal);
30              osc.type = selectedWaveform;
31          }
32      }, 50);
33
```

The remaining changes require you to modify the name of the onOff selector variable to $onOff and replace the addEventListener with the on() method set to respond to click events. Then rename the freqSliderVal to $freqSliderVal, replace the span.innerHTML with $messageText. text(), and lastly replace onOff.value with the JQuery equivalent of $onOff.val().

onOff Method without JQuery

```
app.js          x
73
74      onOff.addEventListener("click", function() {
75
76          if (!osc) {
77              osc = audioContext.createOscillator();
78              osc.type = selectedWaveform;
79              osc.frequency.value = freqSliderVal;
80              osc.connect(audioContext.destination);
81              osc.start(audioContext.currentTime);
82              onOff.value = "stop";
83              span.innerHTML = "Click to stop oscillator";
84          } else {
85
86              osc.stop(audioContext.currentTime);
87              osc = false;
88              onOff.value = "start";
89              span.innerHTML = "Click to start oscillator";
90          }
91      });
```

$onOff Selector with JQuery

```
app.js                                        x

34
35        $onOff.on("click", function() {
36            if (!osc) {
37                osc = audioContext.createOscillator();
38                osc.type = selectedWaveform;
39                osc.frequency.value = $freqSliderVal;
40                osc.connect(audioContext.destination);
41                osc.start(audioContext.currentTime);
42                $onOff.val("stop");
43                $messageText.text("Click to stop oscillator");
44            } else {
45
46                osc.stop(audioContext.currentTime);
47                osc = false;
48                $onOff.val("start");
49                $messageText.text("Click to start oscillator");
50            }
51
52        });
```

Summary

In this chapter, you learned the basics of using JQuery for DOM manipulation. You also refactored the code in the previous chapter to contrast the difference between working with and without JQuery. In the next chapter, you will learn how to import and play back audio files with the Web Audio API.

11 Loading and Playing Audio Files

In this chapter, you will learn the basics of working with audio files. This includes how to load, play, and run audio files through the node graph to take advantage of its built-in effects.

▮ Prerequisites

To load and play back audio files, you must be running a web server. Chapter 1 gives you instructions about how to integrate a web server with Sublime Text by installing a package called Sublime Server. Your audio files are referenced from the directory the web server is pointing to, which you can set up as follows:

1. Create a folder on your desktop with a new project template.

2. Start the Sublime Text web server by selecting *Tools > SublimeServer > Start SublimeServer*.

3. Open the sidebar (if it isn't already open) by selecting *View > Side Bar > Show Side Bar*.

4. Drag the template folder to the side bar panel.

5. Open a web browser and enter: http://localhost:8080 in the URL field.

6. Click the link to the template folder. An empty screen is displayed because the initial template is empty.

   For this exercise, you will need an audio file that is short and preferably of MP3 format (for compatibility issues). The file referenced in the example code is `snare.mp3`. Create a directory in your template folder and name it `sounds`; then copy your MP3 file there.

XMLHttpRequest and Fetch API

There are two built-in browser tools that allow you to load audio files into your applications. The first is called the XMLHttpRequest object and the other is the Fetch API. The Fetch API is a simplified modern abstraction of the XMLHttpRequest object. For this chapter, you will learn how to load audio files using both tools.

The Two Steps to Loading an Audio File

Before you can play audio files using the Web Audio API, you must first load them into your program. After the files are loaded, you can then write additional code to play them back.

Loading an audio file is done in two steps.

1. Request and store the audio file in a buffer using either the XMLHttpRequest Object or Fetch API.

2. Decode the buffer with a method of the AudioContext called `decodeAudioData`.

Loading an Audio File with the XMLHttpRequest Object

In this example, you use the built-in browser object named `XMLHttpRequest` to store the collected audio file in a *buffer*. This object is part of the web browser and is independent of the Web Audio API. A buffer is a small piece of internal memory used to store data so that it can be accessed quickly. Storing the file this way provides low latency playback and the ability to modify the raw waveform data, which is useful for some applications.

In the second step, you use the `decodeAudioData` method to *decode* the audio file buffer. After the Web Audio API has read and decoded the audio data, you can assign the object to a variable and reference it in the node graph for playback.

The following example shows how you load a single audio file, after which you can play it back by clicking on the browser window. A large portion of this

---

11. Loading and Playing Audio Files

chapter is dedicated to explaining each line of the following code and how all the lines work together.

```
const audioContext = new AudioContext();
let audioBuffer;
let getSound = new XMLHttpRequest();
getSound.open("get", "sounds/snare.mp3", true);
getSound.responseType = "arraybuffer";
getSound.onload = function() {
  audioContext.decodeAudioData(getSound.
response, function(buffer) {
    audioBuffer = buffer;
  });
};
getSound.send();
function playback() {
  let playSound = audioContext.createBufferSource();
  playSound.buffer = audioBuffer;
  playSound.connect(audioContext.destination);
  playSound.start(audioContext.currentTime);
}
window.addEventListener("mousedown", playback);
```

The first step is to create a new XMLHttpRequest object. This object allows you to import data over the http protocol, which is the same protocol used to load web pages. This data can then be stored in various forms. The code to create the object is as follows:

```
let getSound = new XMLHttpRequest();
```

The XMLHttpRequest function invocation returns an object literal that is stored in a variable named getSound. This is done using the new keyword. The new keyword will not be covered until the next chapter, but don't worry. For now, the important thing is to understand that XMLHttpRequest is a function that returns an object. This object contains a large collection of built-in properties and methods. For loading sound files, you need five of these methods:

- open

- responseType

- onload

- response

- send

The next line of code uses the open method to fetch the audio file from its respective directory. This method has three arguments.

```
let getSound = new XMLHttpRequest();
getSound.open("get","sound/snare.mp3",true);
```

To clearly understand the purpose of the first argument requires a brief explanation of a command called a get request.

▌ get Requests

When you type a URL into a web browser and "go" to a website, the web browser does not actually go anywhere. What actually happens is the browser issues a command to the website server that initiates a download of the HTML content and other files needed to view it. This command is called a get request. The beauty of get requests is that you can use them outside the context of typing a URL into a browser. In other words, you can write code to run get requests behind the scenes. This is how XMLHttpRequest is used to pull audio files into your application—and why the first argument of the open method is "get".

The second argument to the open method is the path to the file you want to fetch. For this example, an MP3 file named snare.mp3 is imported.

▌ A Word on Audio File Type Compatibility

It is important to understand that audio file type compatibility is dependent on which web browser you use. If you want your application to be compatible with multiple web browsers, you have to include multiple audio files of different formats *and* write conditional code to determine what format to use based on the rendering browser. The three most popular audio file formats for web browsers are WAV, OGG, and MP3. An audio file format compatibility chart for various browsers is available here: http://caniuse.com/#search=audio%20format.

The third argument to the open method determines whether the open operation is done in a synchronous or asynchronous manner. The true value selects the asynchronous setting, whereas false selects the synchronous setting. Understanding the difference between synchronous and asynchronous code execution is an in-depth topic and requires some explaining.

▌ Synchronous versus Asynchronous Code Execution

When the browser executes code, it does so from top to bottom. As a result, a function that takes a long time to execute creates a noticeable delay in the program itself. This is because the code is executing synchronously.

When you use the XMLHttpRequest object to retrieve data *synchronously* from a server, the time delay between making the get request and when the actual data is returned can create a noticeable delay in the execution of your program. This delay is particularly noticeable when you load a large audio file and then have to wait for its entire contents to load into memory before your program continues.

Delays in execution are why doing such operations synchronously is discouraged and doing them *asynchronously* is preferred. Working asynchronously lets you run the open method while immediately allowing your program to continue executing to completion. In the meantime, the audio file continues to load behind the scenes, regardless of how long it takes to complete. When the audio file is available (when it is done loading), you can use it. When code is executed in this manner, we say that it is *nonblocking*. Of course, the downside of this is that if you have an audio file loading and it is taking a long time, the user of your program might be wondering why nothing is playing even though the page has rendered! This problem can be remedied by presenting a message to users to warn them that they will have to wait for the audio file to finish loading. In the meantime, they can explore other parts of your application.

The next line of code sets a property called responseType to a value of arraybuffer. The responseType property defines how the data you are importing is made available to your program. Generally, the XMLHttpRequest object is used to fetch text files, and in those cases you might choose one of the other available responseType settings such as text or document. For sound files, arraybuffer is used. This is a general container for binary data that is useful for audio files.

```
let getSound = new XMLHttpRequest();
getSound.open("get","sounds/snare.mp3",true);
getSound.responseType = "arraybuffer";
```

The next line of code begins with an onload function that is invoked after the data (the audio file) has completed loading. Within the onload function, decoding of the audio data takes place that makes it usable by the Web Audio API. You do this with a method of the AudioContext called decodeAudioData that takes two arguments. The first argument is a property called response that represents the loaded (and *undecoded*) audio data.

```
getSound.onload = function() {
  audioContext.decodeAudioData(getSound.response,
function(buffer) {
    audioBuffer = buffer;
  });
};
```

The second argument to the decodeAudioData method is a callback function that allows you to capture the result of the *decoded* audio data and do something with it. To capture the decoded file, you must pass it as an argument of the callback function. In this case, the name given for this decoded information is buffer. To make buffer accessible to the rest of the program, you can assign it to a global variable.

```
const audioContext = new AudioContext();
let audioBuffer;
let getSound = new XMLHttpRequest();
getSound.open("get", "snare.mp3", true);
getSound.responseType = "arraybuffer";
getSound.onload = function() {
  audioContext.decodeAudioData(getSound.response,
function(buffer) {
```

```
    audioBuffer = buffer; // stored as global variable
  });
};
```

The last line is the send method. This method initiates the XMLHttpRequest.

```
getSound.send();
```

Playing the Audio Content

Now that the audio file is loaded into a buffer, the playback function contains
the required code to connect it to the node graph and eventually play it back. The
first line assigns a method called createBufferSource to a variable. This
method is used to create a *buffer source node* that is used for audio buffers. In
other words, it is like createOscillator, but instead of being used to create
oscillators, it is used to create a node that can play back the contents of an audio
buffer. To inject the audio buffer into the node graph, you need to assign it to a
property of the buffer source node named buffer.

```
function playback() {
  let playSound = audioContext.createBufferSource();
  playSound.buffer = audioBuffer;
  playSound.connect(audioContext.destination);
  playSound.start(audioContext.currentTime);
}
```

You can now connect the buffer to the audioConext.destination and set
the start time.

```
function playback() {
  let playSound = audioContext.createBufferSource();
  playSound.buffer = audioBuffer;
  playSound.connect(audioContext.destination);
  playSound.start(audioContext.currentTime);
}
```

The last line of code is an event listener that lets you play back the file when the
window is clicked.

```
window.addEventListener("mousedown", playback);
```

If you click on the page, you should hear the audio file play.

Processing the Audio Buffer with the Node Graph

When the audio buffer is fed into the node graph, you can process it with its built-
in effects. In the following code, the node graph connection has been modified to
include a property of the audio buffer named playbackRate. This changes the
playback speed of the sound. To double the speed, set the value to 2; to play the
sound back at half speed, set the value to 0.5.

```
function playback() {
  let playSound = audioContext.createBufferSource();
  playSound.buffer = audioBuffer;
  playSound.playbackRate.value = 0.5;
  playSound.connect(audioContext.destination);
  playSound.start(audioContext.currentTime);
}
```

■ Loading Audio Files Using the Fetch API

Loading audio files using the Fetch API requires the same process as the XMLHttpRequest object while using a simplified alternate syntax. Below is a complete working example of how to load files using the fetch API and an explanation of the code.

```
const audioContext = new AudioContext();
let audioBuffer;

fetch("./sounds/snare.mp3")
    .then(data => data.arrayBuffer())
    .then(arrayBuffer => audioContext.decodeAudioData(arrayBuffer))
    .then(decodeAudio=> {
        audioBuffer = decodeAudio
    })

function playback(){
    const playSound = audioContext.createBufferSource();
    playSound.buffer = audioBuffer;
    playSound.connect(audioContext.destination);
    playSound.start(audioContext.currentTime);
}

window.addEventListener("mousedown",playback);
```

To use the Fetch API we use the function called fetch. By default, this function invokes a get request to the specified endpoint. In this case, the endpoint is "./sounds/snare.mp3".

```
fetch("./sounds/snare.mp3")
```

A group of actions is applied to the data using a series of consecutive callbacks via the *then* method. The `then` method is part of an API called the JavaScript promise API. Explaining the JavaScript promise API is beyond the scope of this chapter; however, we will explain the code well enough so that you understand how to load audio files. In short, you can view the `then` methods in the below code as a collection of strung together functions that input, transform, and pass data through one another consecutively.

```
fetch("./sounds/snare.mp3")
    .then(data => data.arrayBuffer())      // 1. get data as array
buffer
    .then(arrayBuffer => audioContext.decodeAudioData(arrayBuffer))
    // 2. decode audio data
```

```
    .then(decodeAudio=> {
        audioBuffer = decodeAudio   // 3. assign decoded audio data to
variable in higher scope.
    })
```

The first callback makes the data available as an array buffer to our program. The second callback takes the array buffer and decodes it making it usable to the Web Audio API. The third callback assigns the decoded audio data to a variable in a higher scope. Each of these actions is performed one after another.

The following code connects the newly created buffer to the audio graph for playback.

```
function playback(){
    const playSound = audioContext.createBufferSource();
    playSound.buffer = audioBuffer;
    playSound.connect(audioContext.destination);
    playSound.start(audioContext.currentTime);
}

window.addEventListener("mousedown",playback);
```

▐ Summary

Each time you want to import an audio file into your program, you must either initiate XMLHttpRequest with all the method and property settings shown in this chapter or use the Fetch API. Although the process is simplified using the Fetch API, you can imagine that duplicating this code repeatedly for each file is unfeasible for a large-scale application. By abstracting away this complexity, you can program a solution to this problem that lets you import multiple audio files with only a few lines of code. In the next two chapters, you will learn how to do this while learning about three new object creation methodologies: factories, constructors, and classes.

12 Factories, Constructors, and Classes

In the previous chapter, you learned how to import audio files. You also learned that loading multiple files can require a tremendous amount of code duplication. Because repeating code is something that should be avoided, it is a good idea to abstract your audio file loading program into a library that imports all the required files with a minimal amount of code duplication. In this chapter, you will learn three new object creation patterns to help you do this. The first pattern, called *factory*, is used to create your audio loader library. The second pattern, called *constructor*, is introduced primarily because of its prevalence in the JavaScript world, making it an important pattern to familiarize yourself with. The third pattern is called *class* and is a syntax that is used in modern JavaScript as an alternative to the constructor pattern. Factories, constructors are classes are almost identical. The difference lies solely in minor implementation details and syntax. In other words, anything you can do with one of these patterns you can do with the other. Your choice of which to use comes down to personal choice.

In the next chapter, you will put what you learn here to work and build your audio file loading library.

DOI: 10.1201/9781003201496-12

JavaScript and the Concept of *Class*

Programming languages that are organized around objects that interact with one another are usually referred to as *object oriented*. JavaScript is considered an object-oriented language, although it differs from traditional object-oriented languages in one important way: JavaScript originally lacked what are called *classes*.

What Are Classes?

With most object-oriented programming languages, to create an object you must first create a class, which is a kind of blueprint that your object is derived from. For example, imagine a class for a mixing console that contains a number of audio channels. When you create an object from this class, you have the option to determine the channel count on the fly. In this regard, the class acts as a kind of scaffolding for the creation of objects while offering a degree of flexibility for individual object customization.

The beauty of JavaScript is that when you create objects *directly*, you do not need classes. However, if you want to program in a class-based style, you can do so easily with three available object creation patterns: factory, constructor, or class.

The Factory Pattern

Factory is a fancy term for describing a function that returns an object.

```
function makeObj() {
  let obj = {};
  return obj;
}
let newObj = makeObj();
```

You can use factories to set properties and methods on the objects they return. In the following example, the factory `makeRecord` is used to create objects that represent music albums. With factories, property values are assigned to the returned object through function arguments. In the following example, the object's property values represent information about each record, including title, artist, and year.

```
function makeRecord(title, artist, year) {
  let  record = {};
  record.title = title;
  record.artist = artist;
  record.year = year;
  return record;
}
let weAreHardcore = makeRecord("We Are Hardcore", "The Psycho
Electros", 2030);
console.log(weAreHardcore.title); // "We Are Hardcore"
console.log(weAreHardcore.artist); // "The Psycho Electros"
console.log(weAreHardcore.year); // 2030
```

If you want to create default values for properties, you can assign them like this:

```
function makeRecord(title, artist, year) {
  let record = {};
  record.title = title;
  record.artist = artist;
  record.year = year;
  record.fullAlbum = true;
  return record;
}
let weAreHardcore = makeRecord("We Are Hardcore",
  "The Psycho Electros", 2030);
console.log(weAreHardcore.fullAlbum); // true
```

You can also include methods in your factories.

```
function makeRecord(title, artist, year) {
  let record = {};
  record.title = title;
  record.artist = artist;
  record.year = year;
  record.summary = function() {
    return "Title:" + record.title + ". Artist:" + record.artist +
      ". Year:" + record.year;
  };
  return record;
}
let weAreHardcore = makeRecord("We Are Hardcore",
  "The Psycho Electros", 2016);
console.log(weAreHardcore.summary()); /*Title:We Are Hardcore.
  Artist:The Psycho Electros. Year:2030*/
```

◼ Dynamic Object Extension

Objects created with factories, like all objects, can be extended to include additional properties and methods. The following example creates a new property named leadSinger and a new method named getAllProperties. getAllProperties loops through the object properties and logs those that are not functions to the console.

```
function makeRecord(title, artist, year) {
  let record = {};
  record.title = title;
  record.artist = artist;
  record.year = year;
  record.summary = function() {
    return "Title:" + record.title + ". Artist:" + record.artist +
      ". Year:" + record.year;
  };
  return record;
}
let weAreHardcore = makeRecord("We Are Hardcore",
  "The Psycho Electros", 2016);
weAreHardcore.leadSinger = "Fred The Butcher";
```

```
weAreHardcore.getAllProperties = function() {
  for (let prop in weAreHardcore) {
    if (typeof weAreHardcore[prop] != "function") {
      //_____Loop ignores methods!
      console.log(prop + ":" + weAreHardcore[prop]);
        //_____Only loops through properties
    }
  }
};
weAreHardcore.getAllProperties();
/*_____RESULT
title:We Are Hardcore
artist:The Psycho Electros
year:2030
leadSinger:Fred The Butcher
_____*/
```

Private Data

Sometimes you want to create data that is accessible to your objects but is either inaccessible to the outside scope or cannot be changed. To do this, you can make data private by assigning it to a variable inside the factory. In the following example, a variable named id stores some private information.

```
function makeRecord(albumId) {
  let id = albumId; // Private data
  console.log(id + " is private data");
  let  record = {};
  return record;
}
let myRecord = makeRecord("2323415432");
console.log(myRecord.albumId); /*undefined. This is a property of the
  object, not the private data!*/
```

Getters and Setters

Private data can be retrieved by creating a method inside the factory that is designed to return it. A method used to retrieve private information is called a *getter*.

```
function makeRecord(albumId) {
  let id = albumId;
  let record = {};
  record.getId = function() { // getter
    return albumId;
  };
  return record;
}
let myRecord = makeRecord("1121210937");
myRecord.getId(); // 1121210937
```

Conversely, methods that are used to modify private data are called *setters*. In the following code, a setter is created that allows you to change the value of id while restricting the input to a ten-digit string.

```
function makeRecord(albumId) {
  let id = albumId;
  let record = {};
  record.getId = function() {
    return id;
  };
  record.setId = function(newId) {
    if (typeof newId === "string" && newId.length === 10) {
      id = newId;
    } else {
      throw ("id must be a ten-digit string");
    }
  };
  return record;
}
let myRecord = makeRecord("9076543210");
myRecord.getId(); // 9876543210
myRecord.setId("1000000001");
myRecord.getId(); // 1000000001
```

Programming with factories is a common pattern in JavaScript and one that you should be sure to familiarize yourself with. Factories give you a simple syntax for abstracting complex code, while offering you the privacy of function scope coupled with the flexibility of object extension.

▮ Constructors and the New Keyword

Another pattern for object creation is called the *constructor*. Like a factory, a constructor is a function that returns an object. The following code shows an implementation of the makeRecord factory using a constructor.

```
function Record(title, artist, year) {
  this.title = title;
  this.artist = artist;
  this.year = year;
}
let weAreHardcore = new Record("We Are Hardcore",
  "The Psycho Electros", 2030);
console.log(weAreHardcore.title); // We Are Hardcore
console.log(weAreHardcore.artist); // The Psycho Electros
console.log(weAreHardcore.year); // 2030
```

As you can see, there are some differences between factories and constructors. The first is the naming convention for functions. With constructors, it is considered good practice to name them with a capitalized *noun*. This convention exists solely to help distinguish constructors from non-constructors and does *not* throw an error if it is not used. The lack of an explicitly created object is the next difference. With constructors, instead of immediately creating an object in your function declaration, begin by writing your properties using the this keyword. In a constructor, this points to the object that is created from it. These properties are assigned values through the constructor function arguments or, if you want to create default values, you can assign them directly to the property.

```
function Record(title, artist, year) {
  this.title = title;
  this.artist = artist;
  this.year = year;
  this.fullAlbum = true; // default value
}
let  weAreHardcore = new Record("We Are Hardcore",
  "The Psycho Electros", 2030);
console.log(weAreHardcore.fullAlbum); // true
```

You invoke a constructor using the new keyword. This is the command that tells the interpreter that you are using the function as a constructor. In response, the interpreter creates and returns an object. In the previous example, the return value is assigned to the variable named weAreHardcore.

▌▌ Adding Methods to Constructors

If you want to add methods to constructors, the syntax looks like this:

```
function Record(title, artist, year) {
  this.title = title;
  this.artist = artist;
  this.year = year;
}
Record.prototype.summary = function() {
  return "Title:" + this.title + ". Artist:" + this.artist +
    ". Year:" + this.year;
};
let  weAreHardcore = new Record("We Are Hardcore", "The Psycho
Electros", 2030);
weAreHardcore.summary(); /*Title:We Are Hardcore. Artist:The Psycho
Electros. Year:2030*/
```

Admittedly, this syntax is a bit odd looking. So, to clarify what is happening, let's look at two concepts interwoven with constructors: the prototype *object* and the prototype *property*.

▌▌ The Prototype Object and the Prototype Property

Every time you create a function in JavaScript, a hidden object gets created in the background that is tied to the function that created it. This object is not visible or accessible and does absolutely nothing *unless* you decide to use your function as a constructor. If you use your function as a constructor, this otherwise dormant object becomes accessible through a property called *prototype* and is called the *prototype object*.

When you attach methods to constructors, you are expected to attach them to the prototype *property*, which in turn attaches them to the hidden prototype *object*. Any objects you create with your constructor have access to these methods.

```
Record.prototype.summary = function() {
```

```
    return "Title:" + this.title + ". Artist:" + this.artist +
      ". Year:" + this.year;
};
```

Although you can attach your methods without using the prototype property, the drawback to this approach is that every time you create a new object, all of the methods are initialized, and this requires more memory. This might have been a concern in 1995 when JavaScript was designed and computers were much slower, but the large amount of available memory in modern computers makes this issue negligible. This is the reason factories are a viable alternative. The syntax for adding methods without using the prototype object looks like this:

```
function Record(title, artist, year) {
  this.title = title;
  this.artist = artist;
  this.year = year;
  this.summary = function() {
    return "Title:" + this.title + ". Artist:" + this.artist +
      ". Year:" + this.year;
  };
}
let  weAreHardcore = new Record("We Are Hardcore", "The Psycho
Electros", 2016);
weAreHardcore.summary();  /*Title:We Are Hardcore. Artist:The
Psycho Electros. Year:2030*/
```

You can use getters and setters, as you do with factories, to work with private data in constructors. The following example contains a private variable named id and uses a getter to retrieve it, as well as a setter that allows it to be changed to a ten-digit string. Note that the getter and setter are not implemented on the prototype property, because if they were, the private data would not be available to them.

```
function Record(albumId) {
  let  id = albumId;
  this.getId = function() {
    return id;
  };
  this.setId = function(newId) {
    if (typeof newId === "string" && newId.length === 10) {
      id = newId;
    } else {
      throw ("id must be a ten digit string");
    }
  };
}
let  myRecord = new Record("9876543210");
myRecord.getId(); // 9876543210
myRecord.setId("0123456789");
myRecord.getId(); //0123456789
```

Why Do Constructors Exist If You Can Do the Same Thing with Factories?

At the time when JavaScript was developed in 1995, one of the most popular languages in the world was Java. Out of a desire to appease Java developers and lure them into using JavaScript, the language was designed to mirror Java's syntax. Part of this effort included adding constructors to the language that were designed to *look like* Java classes. This happened irrespective of the fact that behind-the-scenes JavaScript was not a class-based language.

Web Audio API Nodes Can Be Written in Constructor Syntax

The Web Audio API has constructor functions that can be used in place of their factory equivalents. Below is an example of creating an oscillator node using constructor syntax.

```
let audioContext = new AudioContext();
let options = {
frequency:150,
type:"sawtooth"
}
let osc = new OscillatorNode(audioContext,options);
```

According to the Mozilla Developer network, this newer constructor syntax is the preferred style for writing Web Audio API code. The factory style will never be deprecated and the future of the Web Audio API specification will allow for both styles. For this book, I opted to use the factory style as I believe it is easier to understand for beginners.

Classes

The final object creation pattern discussed in this chapter is the class pattern. Classes are a later edition to the language and were added in 2015. I have reserved the class pattern to explain last because factories and constructors make apparent what classes do behind the scenes. If you understand factories and constructors, classes are easier to grasp

Classes in JavaScript Are Just Constructors with a Different Syntax

When you create a class in JavaScript you are really just using an alternate syntax to implement the constructor pattern. Behind the scenes, "classes" are technically implemented as constructors. You might be wondering why were classes added to the language in the first place. Classes were added to the language because they are a common pattern among other object-oriented languages, thus making the language easier for programmers of those other languages.

▌ A Class Example

To demonstrate class syntax, we convert the previous constructor example named Record into a class. The example is below.

First, we start with the constructor version.

```
// Constructor
function Record(title, artist, year) {
    this.title = title;
    this.artist = artist;
    this.year = year;
}

Record.prototype.summary = function() {
    return "Title:" + this.title + ". Artist:" + this.artist + ".
Year:" + this.year;
};

let weAreHardcore = new Record("We Are Hardcore", "The Psycho
Electros", 2030);
weAreHardcore.summary();   // Title:We Are Hardcore. Artist:The
Psycho Electros. Year:2030
```

Next, we create a version of the previous code using the equivalent class syntax.

```
class Record{
    constructor(title, artist, year){
        this.title = title;
        this.artist = artist;
        this.year = year;
    }

    summary(){
        return "Title:" + this.title + ". Artist:" + this.artist +
". Year:" + this.year;
    }
}

let weAreHardcore = new Record("We Are Hardcore", "The Psycho
Electros", 2030);
weAreHardcore.summary(); //Title:We Are Hardcore. Artist:The Psycho
Electros. Year:2030
```

When creating a class, *declare* the class by writing the class keyword. You then type the name of the class and write a pair of opening and closing curly braces to encapsulate the class body.

```
Class Record {
}
```

The next step is to compose the constructor method of the class. In a class, the constructor method is where you write object properties. The constructor method

---

of a class is similar to the body of a constructor function in that they both use the "this" keyword to point to the properties of newly created objects.

```
class Record{
    constructor(title, artist, year){
        this.title = title;
        this.artist = artist;
        this.year = year;
    }
}
```

To create a new object, you do so by invoking the new keyword and using the same syntax as the constructor pattern.

```
let weAreHardcore = new Record("We Are Hardcore", "The Psycho
Electros", 2030);
console.log(weAreHardcore);
/*
    {
        title: 'We Are Hardcore',
        artist: 'The Psycho Electros',
        year: 2030
    }
*/
```

To create methods, you place them in the body of the class as shown in the example below.

```
class Record{
    constructor(title, artist, year){
        this.title = title;
        this.artist = artist;
        this.year = year;
    }
    summary(){              // class method syntax
        return "Title:" + this.title + ". Artist:" + this.artist +
". Year:" + this.year;
    }
}

let weAreHardcore = new Record("We Are Hardcore", "The Psycho
Electros", 2030);
weAreHardcore.summary(); // Title:We Are Hardcore. Artist:The
Psycho Electros. Year:2030
```

▮ Private Data and Classes

To create private data in classes you use hash names. A hash is the symbol #and a *hash name* is an identifier that uses the #name syntax to identify properties of a class that are private. In the code below, the #id at the top of the class identifies a private property named #id. In the constructor portion of the code, the #id value is set when an object is created from the class.

```
class Record{
    #id;     // Identifies property as private
    constructor(recordId){
        this.#id = recordId // Private property is set when object
is created.
    }
}
```

When an object is created, any attempt to access private properties directly results in an error.

```
let app = new Record("8wy45hw934jd9yct9ydtx79tdy");
console.log(app.#id) // error , data is private.
```

To retrieve or change private property values, you must use specialized methods prefaced with the keywords get and set. The following example contains a method named currentId that is prefaced with the get keyword to retrieve the private #id information.

```
class Record{
    #id;
    constructor(recordId){
        this.#id = recordId
    }
    get currentId() {
      return this.#id;
    }
}
```

```
let app = new Record("8wy45hw934jd9yct9ydtx79tdy");
console.log(app.currentId);   // 8wy45hw934jd9yct9ydtx79tdy
```

The code below demonstrates how to change private properties using methods prefaced with the set keyword.

```
class Record{
    #id;
    constructor(recordId){
        this.#id = recordId
    }

    get currentId() {
      return this.#id;
    }

    set createNewId(newId){
        this.#id = newId;
    }
}
```

```
let app = new Record("8wy45hw934jd9yct9ydtx79tdy");

app.createNewId = "xyz123"
console.log(app.currentId);   // xyz123
```

■ Summary

In this chapter, you learned how to create JavaScript classes and pseudo classes using factories and constructors. In the next chapter, you will create a simplified audio file loader library using the factory pattern.

13 Abstracting the File Loader

Now that you are familiar with factories and constructors from the previous chapter, you can abstract the audio buffer loader you created in Chapter 11 into a library that loads multiple sound files using less code. You do this using the factory pattern.

▊ Thinking about Code Abstraction

Organizing your code into abstractions can be a daunting task. However, there are two steps you can follow to simplify the process. The first step is to determine whether you need an abstraction in the first place. If you are repeatedly typing out a large amount of code for the same task, then the answer is probably *yes*. The second step, if you decide you need an abstraction, is to determine what type of interface works for your abstraction. You were exposed to one example of a popular interface in Chapter 11, where you worked with the JQuery library. JQuery's interface allows you to treat HTML elements as objects that you can attach methods to. This is an excellent choice for an interface, but sometimes a simple function invocation that returns a string or number works just as well. Ultimately, it depends on your objective and the nature of the code you are abstracting.

One way to help you decide on the best approach is to work backward and *write out how you would like the interface to look and function prior to implementing it.* The interface for the audio file abstraction you create in this chapter looks like the following example:

```
let sound = audioBatchLoader({
  kick: "sounds/kick.mp3",
  snare: "sounds/snare.mp3",
  hihat: "sounds/hihat.mp3",
  shaker: "sounds/shaker.mp3"
});
sound.snare.play(); // Play
```

With this approach, a factory function takes an object as an argument. The object you input into the factory contains a list of property names, each of which is assigned a directory of an audio file in the form of a string. The beauty of this approach is its clarity and extensibility. The interface shown in `sound.snare.play()` attempts to read, somewhat like English, from the list of sound files to play. Even if you have never seen this code before, you can understand what it is doing: selecting a sound in a specified directory and playing it. Decoupling the object that contains many audio files from the invoking function makes the code easier to read, as shown in the following example:

```
let audioFiles = {
  kick: "kick.mp3",
  snare: "snare.mp3",
  hihat: "hihat.mp3",
  shaker: "shaker.mp3"
  //_____hundreds of audio files could be listed here........
};
let sound = audioBatchLoader(audioFiles);
sound.snare.play(); // Play
```

If the user of your abstraction decides they want to extend it to do new things, without having to modify the source code in the original function, they have some flexibility. So for example, if they wanted to extend the returned object to play multiple audio buffers, they could do this:

```
sound.playSnareAndShaker = function() {
  sound.snare.play();
  sound.shaker.play();
};
sound.playSnareAndShaker(); // plays two sounds at the same time
with one line of code
```

▌ Creating the Abstraction

The following code is the *finished* abstraction. The remainder of this chapter is dedicated to building up this example line by line and explaining how it works. Create a new template project and save the following code in the JavaScript folder in a file named `audiolib.js`.

```
"use strict";
const audioContext = new AudioContext();
function audioFileLoader(fileDirectory) {
```

```
    let soundObj = {};
    let playSound = undefined;
    let getSound = new XMLHttpRequest();
    soundObj.fileDirectory = fileDirectory;
    getSound.open("GET", soundObj.fileDirectory, true);
    getSound.responseType = "arraybuffer";
    getSound.onload = function() {
        audioContext.decodeAudioData(getSound.response,
function(buffer) {
            soundObj.soundToPlay = buffer;
        });

    };

    getSound.send();

    soundObj.play = function(time, setStart, setDuration) {
        playSound = audioContext.createBufferSource();
        playSound.buffer = soundObj.soundToPlay;
        playSound.connect(audioContext.destination);
        playSound.start(audioContext.currentTime + time ||
audioContext.currentTime, setStart || 0, setDuration || soundObj.
soundToPlay.duration);
    };
    soundObj.stop = function(time) {

        playSound.stop(audioContext.currentTime + time ||
audioContext.currentTime);

    };
    return soundObj;

}

function audioBatchLoader(obj) {
    for (let prop in obj) {
        obj[prop] = audioFileLoader(obj[prop]);
    }
    return obj;
}
```

You now need to reference the file in your index.html file.

```
<head>
  <meta charset="UTF-8">
  <title></title>
  <script src="js/audiolib.js"></script>
  <script src="js/app.js"></script>
  <link rel="stylesheet" href="css/app.css">
</head>
```

The below code is used to load and play sound files and can be placed in app.js

```
let sound = audioBatchLoader({
  kick: "sounds/kick.mp3",
  snare: "sounds/snare.mp3",
  hihat: "sounds/hihat.mp3",
```

```
  shaker: "sounds/shaker.mp3"
});
window.addEventListener("mousedown", function() {
  sound.snare.play();
});
```

Create a folder named sounds. This is the directory used to hold your audio files.

You can use your own audio files or use the audio files included in the example code for this chapter.

Run sublime server and click the opening page. The audio file named snare. mp3 will play. If you do not include the sound files, you will get an error.

▉ Walking through the Code

The function named audioFileLoader creates and returns an object named soundObj.

```
function audioFileLoader(){
  let soundObj = {};
  return soundObj;
};
```

To specify a directory for the file to be used, a parameter is assigned to a property of soundObj named fileDirectory.

```
function audioFileLoader(fileDirectory){
  let soundObj = {};

let playSound = undefined;
```

```
  soundObj.fileDirectory = fileDirectory;
  return soundObj;
};
```

You can now create the XMLHttpRequest object and set all the required properties and methods. You can also implement the decodeAudioData method to make the buffer usable by the Web Audio API. These lines of code should already be familiar to you because they are the same buffer loading and decoding tools you learned about in Chapter 11, with one small difference. In Chapter 11, the decoded buffer was assigned to a variable named audioBuffer. In this implementation, the decoded buffer is assigned to a property of soundObj named soundBuffer.

```
function audioFileLoader(fileDirectory) {
  let soundObj = {};
  let playSound = undefined;
  let getSound = new XMLHttpRequest();
  soundObj.fileDirectory = fileDirectory;
  getSound.open("GET", soundObj.fileDirectory, true);
  getSound.responseType = "arraybuffer";
  getSound.onload = function() {
    audioContext.decodeAudioData(getSound.
response, function(buffer) {
      soundObj.soundToPlay = buffer; // Property assigned buffer
    });
  };
  getSound.send();
  return soundObj;
}
```

You can now create a playback method that is an extension of soundObj to play back the buffers.

```
function audioFileLoader(fileDirectory) {
  let soundObj = {};
  let playSound = undefined;
  soundObj.fileDirectory = fileDirectory;
  let getSound = new XMLHttpRequest();
  getSound.open("GET", soundObj.fileDirectory, true);
  getSound.responseType = "arraybuffer";
  getSound.onload = function() {
    audioContext.decodeAudioData(getSound.
response, function(buffer) {
      soundObj.soundToPlay = buffer;
    });
  };
  getSound.send();
  soundObj.play = function(time) {
    playSound = audioContext.createBufferSource();
    playSound.buffer = soundObj.soundToPlay;
    playSound.connect(audioContext.destination);
    playSound.start(audioContext.currentTime + time ||
      audioContext.currentTime);
  };
  return soundObj;
}
```

The time argument of the play function determines the number of seconds you want the audio file to play into the future. The logical expression (audio-Context.currentTime + time || audioContext.currentTime) is used to determine whether the time argument is empty and, if it is, then the start method does not add additional seconds to the value of audioContext.currentTime. When no arguments are set, the sound plays immediately.

```
soundObj.play = function(time) {
  playSound = audioContext.createBufferSource();
  playSound.buffer = soundObj.soundToPlay;
  playSound.connect(audioContext.destination);
  playSound.start(audioContext.currentTime + time ||
    audioContext.currentTime);
};
```

The stop method lets users determine when a sound will stop playback.

```
const audioContext = new AudioContext();
function audioFileLoader(fileDirectory) {
    let soundObj = {};
    let playSound = undefined;
    soundObj.fileDirectory = fileDirectory;
    let getSound = new XMLHttpRequest();
    getSound.open("GET", soundObj.fileDirectory, true);
    getSound.responseType = "arraybuffer";
    getSound.onload = function() {
        audioContext.decodeAudioData(getSound.response,
function(buffer) {
            soundObj.soundToPlay = buffer;
        });
    };
    getSound.send();
    soundObj.play = function(time) {
        playSound = audioContext.createBufferSource();
        playSound.buffer = soundObj.soundToPlay;
        playSound.connect(audioContext.destination);
        playSound.start(audioContext.currentTime + time ||
            audioContext.currentTime);
    };

    soundObj.stop = function(time) {
        playSound.stop(audioContext.currentTime + time ||
            audioContext.currentTime);
    }
    return soundObj;
}
```

You can now load the files and play them.

```
let sound = audioFileLoader("sounds/snare.mp3");
window.addEventListener("mousedown", function() {
  sound.play(); // plays at "current time" because no arguments are
set
  sound.play(2); // plays 2 seconds into the future
});
```

This code works, but it reveals a new potential problem. If you want to load multiple files, you have to type out an audioFileLoader invocation for each one, like this:

```
let kick = audioFileLoader("sounds/kick.mp3");
let snare = audioFileLoader("sounds/snare.mp3");
let hihat = audioFileLoader("sounds/hihat.mp3");
let shaker = audioFileLoader("sounds/shaker.mp3");
```

One way to mitigate this additional repetition is to create a helper function that loops through an object that contains a collection of audio file directories and invokes the audioFileloader on each file. You can then return the object. This will allow each sound to be accessible via its property name. The following code demonstrates this:

```
function audioBatchLoader(obj) {
  for (let prop in obj) {
    obj[prop] = audioFileLoader(obj[prop]);
  }
  return obj;
}
```

You now load multiple files using this code.

```
let sound = audioBatchLoader({
  kick: "sounds/kick.mp3",
  snare: "sounds/snare.mp3",
  hihat: "sounds/hihat.mp3",
  shaker: "sounds/shaker.mp3"
});
```

Each file is now accessible using the following syntax:

```
sound.kick.play();
sound.snare.play();
sound.hihat.play();
sound.shaker.play();
```

You now have a working library to load multiple audio files. The following code sets an event listener on the window. If you click it, you will hear the loaded sound play.

```
let sound = audioBatchLoader({
  kick: "sounds/kick.mp3",
  snare: "sounds/snare.mp3",
  hihat: "sounds/hihat.mp3",
  shaker: "sounds/shaker.mp3"
});
window.addEventListener("mousedown", function() {
  sound.snare.play();
});
```

▮ Summary

In this chapter, you learned the basics of how to think about abstraction, while creating a new tool for loading and playing back multiple audio files. In the next few chapters, you will learn how to manipulate audio via the node graph using various effects.

14 The Node Graph and Working with Effects

Up to this point, the topic of the *node graph* has only been partially described and has been used mostly as a tool to explain related concepts. In this chapter, you will learn how to work with the node graph to develop custom signal chains for complex audio applications. The Web Audio API includes many built-in objects that let you manipulate audio in creative ways. You also learn how to include these objects in your applications and use them to create customized effects.

■ How to *Think About* the Node Graph

In a real-world recording studio, you route audio signals by connecting microphones and other sound sources to a sound mixer. The sound mixer is configured with its own routing scheme, which allows access to equalizers, dynamics processors, and other effects. The Web Audio API node graph is designed to mirror the characteristics of a real-world sound mixer. This is done by connecting input sources such as oscillators and audio buffers to other objects that manipulate the sonic characteristics of these input sources in some way. The various objects (including the input sources) that make up the signal chains are called *nodes* and are connected to one another using a method named connect(). You can think of connect() as a virtual audio cable used to chain the output of one node to the input of another node. The final endpoint connection for any Web Audio application is always going to be the audioContext.destination. You can think of the `audioContext.destination` as the *speakers* of your application. This collection of connections is what is referred to as the *node graph*, shown in the figure below.

❚ Gain Nodes

In a real-world recording studio, you typically use a sound mixer with multiple channel strips and a routing matrix to split and combine audio signals. With the Web Audio API node graph, you use *gain nodes* to split and combine *input sources*. Gain nodes allow independent volume control over input sources and act as virtual mixing channels.

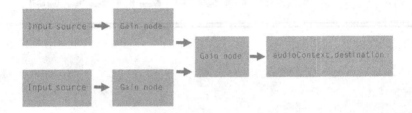

The following code is an example of creating two oscillators and connecting each one to an independent gain node for individual volume control. These are summed to a third gain node, which is connected to the `audioContext.destination`.

```
//_____BEGIN create sawtooth oscillator
let oscSaw = audioContext.createOscillator();
oscSaw.type = "sawtooth";
oscSaw.frequency.value = 118;
oscSaw.start(audioContext.currentTime);

//_____END create sawtooth oscillator

/*_____BEGIN create gain node and
  connect sawtooth oscillator*/
let gainSaw = audioContext.createGain();
gainSaw.gain.value = 0.6; // set volume
oscSaw.connect(gainSaw);

/*_____END create gain node and connect
  sawtooth oscillator*/

/*_____BEGIN create triangle wave
  oscillator*/
let oscTri = audioContext.createOscillator();
```

```
oscTri.type = "triangle";
oscTri.frequency.value = 120;
oscTri.start(audioContext.currentTime);

/*_____END create triangle wave
   oscillator*/

/*_____BEGIN create gain node and
   connect triangle wave oscillator*/
let gainTri = audioContext.createGain();
gainTri.gain.value = 3; // set volume
oscTri.connect(gainTri);

/*_____END create gain node and connect
   triangle wave oscillator*/
//____SUM both Oscillators___
let gainOscSum = audioContext.createGain();
gainOscSum.gain.value = 1;
gainTri.connect(gainOscSum);
gainSaw.connect(gainOscSum);
//____Connect to the audioContext.destination
gainOscSum.connect(audioContext.destination);
```

▍ The Placement of Nodes Is Up to You

It is important to realize that due to the flexible nature of the node graph, you can
place your input sources and other nodes at any part of the chain. Imagine you
have ten gain nodes all connected in series, and you want to inject an oscillator
into the sixth one. This is perfectly fine because the oscillator is unaffected by
the first five gain nodes in the chain by being funneled through the last five gain
nodes prior to reaching the audioContext.destination. This is not just a
feature of gain nodes but the nature of the node graph. *You can place any input
source, or any other node, anywhere you want in the node graph signal chain.* The
order in which you connect objects is dependent on the result you want.

▍ What Effects Are Available?

The following chart contains some of the nodes that are characteristic of the
effect processors you see in real-world recording studios. These effects are called
modification nodes, but for clarity, they are referred to as *effects nodes* in this
book. The specifics of effects nodes are explored in later chapters. The focus of
this chapter is to give you a general understanding of how these effects nodes can
be incorporated into the node graph.

Node Name	Effect	Description
Gain	Volume modification	Sets the volume of an input source. Gain nodes are also used as virtual mixing channels that can be connected in parallel or in series
StereoPanner	2D equal power panning	Changes the stereo placement of sound in 2D space
BiquadFilter	EQ filter	Accentuates or attenuates part of the frequency spectrum of an input source
Delay	Audible delay	Creates a time delay between when an input source plays and when the signal is made audible
Convolver	Convolution reverberation	Creates reverberation effects by referencing impulse response files that model real-world spaces. Can also be used creatively for nonreverb applications
DynamicsCompressor	Dynamic range compression	Modifies the volume of a signal dynamically

How to Determine the Nodes You Need to Create the Effect You Want

If you have an idea for an effect you want to incorporate into your application, you can follow these steps to help determine the tools you need to create it:

1. Determine the specific type of effect you want (chorus, tremolo, hall reverberation, multiband, EQ, etc.).

2. Determine the nature of the effect. In other words, if the effect you want is a chorus, then the nature of the effect is an audible delay. If the effect you want is a multiband equalizer, then the nature of the effect is audio filtering.

3. Research the Web Audio API specification to find a node that you can use to create the effect. Many times, creating the exact effect you want requires combining different nodes or combining similar nodes with slightly modified parameters.

4. Invoke the respective method of the `AudioContext` to create the node (or nodes if you are using more than one). This is a method that starts with the word *create*, such as `createGain()` or `createBiquadFilter()`.

5. Connect the object (or objects if you are using more than one) to the node graph in the part of the signal chain that you want.

6. Modify the built-in properties and methods of the object(s) to manipulate the input source(s) in the manner you want.

A Real-World Example

Assume you want to apply a low-pass (also called *lowpass*) filter to an oscillator. (A low-pass filter is a filter that only allows signals below a certain frequency to pass.) To do this, you first research the Web Audio API documentation to see whether this type of filter is supported. You can search the specification directly at: https://www.w3.org/TR/webaudio. An alternative reference (and one that is a bit more readable) is the Mozilla Developer Network documentation at: https://developer.mozilla.org/en-US/docs/Web/API/Web_Audio_API.

When researching, do a search for "filters" or "lowpass". In the results, you will discover that there is a specialized node called a *biquad filter* that is dedicated to audio filtering. This node includes a property named `type` that you can set to `lowpass`. As the value implies, this filter type is used to apply a low-pass filter to an input source. To apply this to your application, you first invoke the `createBiquadFilter()` method, which returns an object that you store in a variable. You then connect an input source, such as an oscillator or array buffer, to this object using the `connect` method.

```
const audioContext = new AudioContext();
let osc = audioContext.createOscillator();
osc.start(audioContext.currentTime);
let filter = audioContext.createBiquadFilter();
filter.type = "lowpass";
osc.connect(filter);
filter.connect(audioContext.destination);
```

The final step is to define any additional properties or methods to customize the effect. Properties or methods that allow you to customize the behavior of nodes are called *audio params* (short for *audio parameters*). In the previous example, `type` is an audio param. The following code sets another audio param named `frequency` to the value 250. This defines where the low-pass filter begins to cut off in the frequency spectrum.

```
const audioContext = new AudioContext();
let osc = audioContext.createOscillator();
osc.start(audioContext.currentTime);
let filter = audioContext.createBiquadFilter();
filter.type = "lowpass"; // audio param
filter.frequency.value = 250; // audio param
osc.connect(filter);
filter.connect(audioContext.destination);
```

Some Effects Require Development Work

It is important to understand that the Web Audio API's effects nodes are *building blocks*. This means that some of the effects you want to achieve might require additional development work on your part. For example, if you want to use a multiband equalizer, you won't find a "multiband equalizer node" in the Web Audio API specification. Instead, you must build your own multiband equalizer using a collection of `BiquadFilter` nodes.

◼ Summary

In this chapter, you were formally introduced to the node graph and how to create custom signal chains using input sources and effects nodes. In the next few chapters, you will build on this knowledge and explore the specifics of some of these effects nodes.

15 Adding Flexibility to the Audio Loader Abstraction

In this chapter, you will add flexibility to the audio loader abstraction and give users independently customizable node graphs for audio buffer input sources. In its current state, the audio loader library you created in Chapter 13 loads customized sounds but does not allow for customized node graphs for individual audio files. This is undesirable for two reasons. The first is that when you create a library, you don't want the user to have to modify its internals to get the functionality they want. The second reason is that it is useful to have the choice to apply completely different effects to different audio input sources, which requires node configurations that are independently customizable. In this chapter, you will add flexibility to the audio loader abstraction and give users independently customizable node graphs for audio buffer input sources.

▐█ The Problem

If you want to create independent node graphs using the audio loader abstraction you can do so by accessing the buffers directly. The downside to this approach is that playing them back requires some code duplication.

```
let sound = audioBatchLoader({
    snare: "sounds/snare.mp3",    // <---remember these are buffers!
    kick: "sounds/kick.mp3",
```

DOI: 10.1201/9781003201496-15

```
        hihat: "sounds/hihat.mp3"
});

    //_____BEGIN custom node graph
function playSnare(){
    let playSound = audioContext.createBufferSource(); //Didn't we
already code this in the library?
    playSound.buffer = sound.snare.soundToPlay;             // Assign
buffer
    playSound.start(audioContext.currentTime);             // Play
sound
    playSound.connect(audioContext.destination);        // Connect
to node output
}
    //_____END custom node graph


window.addEventListener("mousedown", function() {
    playSnare();
});
```

To fix this problem, we will make a small change to our library ensuring each
loaded audio file can reference its own custom node graph and to do so using
less code than the previous example. The update will introduce a new custom
method named connect. Our connect method is not to be confused with the
built-in connect() method of the Web Audio API and is used for our library
specifically. The use case of our newly created connect method is expressed in the
following example.

```
let sound = audioBatchLoader({
    snare: "sounds/snare.mp3",
    kick: "sounds/kick.mp3",
    hihat: "sounds/hihat.mp3"
});


//_____BEGIN custom node graph
function customNodeGraph(sound){
    let gain = audioContext.createGain();
    gain.gain.value = 0.5;
    sound.connect(gain);
    gain.connect(audioContext.destination);
}

//_____END custom node graph

window.addEventListener("mousedown", function() {
    sound.snare.connect(customNodeGraph).play();

});
```

One thing to keep in mind is that even though this update makes individualized
node graphs easier, there are times when you might need to create a node graph

where audio buffers affect one another. In those cases, you can either revert back to working with audio buffers directly or create more tedious abstractions that are beyond the scope of this book.

■ Complete Working Library Update Incorporating Node Graph Code

```
"use strict";
const audioContext = new AudioContext();
function audioFileLoader(fileDirectory) {
    let soundObj = {};
    let playSound = undefined;
    let getSound = new XMLHttpRequest();
    soundObj.fileDirectory = fileDirectory;
    getSound.open("GET", soundObj.fileDirectory, true);
    getSound.responseType = "arraybuffer";
    getSound.onload = function() {
        audioContext.decodeAudioData(getSound.response,
function(buffer) {
            soundObj.soundToPlay = buffer;

        });
    };

    getSound.send();

    //_____START update custom connect method

    let nodeGraph;

    soundObj.connect = function(callback) {
        if (callback) {
            nodeGraph = callback;
        }
        return {
            play: soundObj.play,
            stop: soundObj.stop
        }
    }

    //_____END update


    soundObj.play = function(time) {
        playSound = audioContext.createBufferSource();
        playSound.buffer = soundObj.soundToPlay;
        playSound.connect(audioContext.destination);   // Remove
        this line
        playSound.start(audioContext.currentTime + time ||
audioContext.currentTime);

        //_____START update to insert
custom node graph as callback
```

```
        if (nodeGraph) {
            return nodeGraph(playSound);
        } else {
            return playSound.connect(audioContext.destination);
        }

        //_____END update

    };

    soundObj.stop = function(time) {
        playSound.stop(audioContext.currentTime + time ||
audioContext.currentTime);
    };
    return soundObj;
}

function audioBatchLoader(obj) {
    for (let prop in obj) {
        obj[prop] = audioFileLoader(obj[prop]);
    }
    return obj;
}
```

The explanation of the code is as follows. We first attach a method named connect to the soundObj object. The connect method takes a callback as a parameter and has a body with a conditional statement checking for the existence of the callback. When the callback is passed, it is assigned to a variable in a higher scope named nodeGraph. If the callback is omitted, the else branch of the conditional statement is run and the connect method simply returns the play and stop methods previously implemented. The code contained within the else branch ensures the sound will still play and stop as expected even if our connect method is invoked with no callback.

```
    let nodeGraph;
    soundObj.connect = function(callback) {
        if (callback) {    // If callback is passed in assign it to
variable in higher scope named nodeGraph.
            nodeGraph = callback;
        }
        return {            // If callback is omitted then simply
return play and stop methods.
            play: soundObj.play,
            stop: soundObj.stop
        }
    }


/* If the following code is run, the sound will still play even
though the callback is omitted from the connect method. */
sound.snare.connect().play() ;
```

The next change is an update to the play method. In this part of the code, you create a conditional statement checking that the nodeGraph variable is assigned a value.

If true, the soundObj.play method returns the invoked nodeGraph() function and passes it the audio buffer as an argument, therefore injecting a node graph into the control flow of sound file playback. If the nodeGraph variable is unassigned then playSound.connect(audioContext destination) is returned and no custom node graph code is injected into the sound file playback code.

```
soundObj.play = function(time) {
    playSound = audioContext.createBufferSource();
    playSound.buffer = soundObj.soundBuffer;
    playSound.start(audioContext.currentTime + time ||
audioContext.currentTime);

    //_____START update to insert
custom node graph as callback

    if (nodeGraph) {
        return nodeGraph(playSound);
    } else {
        return playSound.connect(audioContext.destination);
    }

    //_____END update

};
```

If you've done everything correctly the library works as expected.

```
let sound = audioBatchLoader({
    snare: "sounds/snare.mp3",
    kick: "sounds/kick.mp3",
    hihat: "sounds/hihat.mp3"
});

//_____BEGIN custom node graph
function customNodeGraph(sound) {
    let gain = audioContext.createGain();
    gain.gain.value = 0.5;
    sound.connect(gain);
    gain.connect(audioContext.destination);
}
//_____END custom node graph

window.addEventListener("mousedown", function() {
    sound.snare.connect(customNodeGraph).play();
});
```

▍ Summary

In this chapter, you added additional flexibility to your audio loader library and in the process, you were exposed to a real-world example of how callback functions can be useful when designing a library. In the next chapter, you will continue to learn about node graphs.

16

The Biquad Filter Node

One of the most common ways to manipulate sound is by boosting or attenuating a range of frequencies using audio filters. A familiar example of this is the use of audio equalizers to brighten or muffle a sound. The Web Audio API has a node named `BiquadFilter` that allows you to create different types of audio filters that can be connected together to create various forms of equalizers. In this chapter, you will learn how to use the `BiquadFilter` node, and in the process, you will create a seven-band graphic equalizer and a single-band parametric equalizer.

▮ Using the Biquad Filter Node

To use the `BiquadFilter` node, you must first instantiate it using the `create BiquadFilter` function and store the returned object in a variable.

```
const audioContext = new AudioContext();
let filter = audioContext.createBiquadFilter();
```

Once you create the object, you can connect an input source to it. The following example connects an oscillator to the object.

```
let audioContext = new AudioContext();
let osc = audioContext.createOscillator();
```

DOI: 10.1201/9781003201496-16

```
let filter = audioContext.createBiquadFilter();
osc.connect(filter); // connect input source to filter
osc.start(audioContext.currentTime);
filter.connect(audioContext.destination); /*connect filter to
  audioContext.destination*/
```

▮▮ Filter Types

BiquadFilter contains a property named type that defines the type of filter
the node behaves like. If you do not explicitly set the type property, its default
value is lowpass. You can see this in the console.log() output in the following code:

```
const audioContext = new AudioContext();
let osc = audioContext.createOscillator();
let filter = audioContext.createBiquadFilter();
filter.frequency.value = 250;
console.log(filter.type); // default is lowpass
osc.connect(filter);
osc.start(audioContext.currentTime);
filter.connect(audioContext.destination);
```

To explicitly set the type property to lowpass, you write the following code:

```
filter.type = "lowpass";
```

In addition to the type property, BiquadFilter has a property named
frequency.value that allows you to assign a particular frequency to the
object. The value is in hertz and is represented by a number. The default value
is 350.

```
filter.frequency.value = 1000; // 1000 Hz or 1 kHz
```

The type value of a BiquadFilter node determines if it has two additional
properties: gain and Q. The gain.value property allows you to boost or attenuate frequency.value. The Q.value property represents the bandwidth
of the frequency value. Bandwidth represents the reach by which neighboring
frequencies are affected in relation to changes made to the gain of the selected
frequency. The following images demonstrate the difference between a narrow
bandwidth setting and a wide bandwidth setting of a 1 kHz frequency using a
peaking filter.

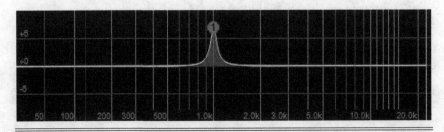

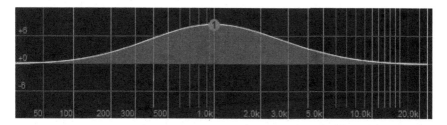

The effect `Q.value` and `gain.value` have on `frequency.value` depends on the filter's `type` setting. The following chart lists the available filter types and describes the relationship between `type`, `frequency`, `Q`, and `gain` properties.

Type	Description	Frequency	Q	Gain
`lowpass`	Frequencies below the cutoff are allowed to pass through. Frequencies above the cutoff are attenuated.	The cutoff frequency.	The larger the value, the greater the peak produced.	*Not used*
`highpass`	Frequencies above the cutoff are allowed to pass through. Frequencies below the cutoff are attenuated.	The cutoff frequency.	Sets the width of the frequency band. The greater the number, the narrower the value.	*Not used*
`bandpass`	Frequencies inside the range of frequencies pass through. Frequencies outside the range are attenuated.	The center of the range of frequencies.	Sets the width of the frequency band. The greater the number, the narrower the value.	*Not used*
`lowshelf`	Frequencies lower than the upper limit get a boost or an attenuation depending on the gain setting.	The upper limit of the frequencies receiving the boost or attenuation.	*Not used*	Creates a boost in decibel. If the value is negative, the gain is attenuated.
`highshelf`	Frequencies higher than the lower limit get a boost or an attenuation depending on the gain setting.	The lower limit of the frequencies getting a boost or an attenuation.	*Not used*	Creates a boost in decibel. If the value is negative, the gain is attenuated.

(Continued)

Type	Description	Frequency	Q	Gain
peaking	Frequencies inside a range of frequencies are boosted or attenuated depending on the gain setting.	The middle of the frequency range getting a boost or an attenuation.	Sets the width of the frequency band. The greater the number, the narrower the value.	Creates a boost in decibel. If the value is negative, the gain is attenuated.
notch	Frequencies inside a range of frequencies are not allowed to pass through.	The center of the range of frequencies.	Controls the width of the frequency band. The greater the Q value, the smaller the frequency band produced.	*Not used*
allpass	Allows all frequencies through but changes their phase relationship.	The frequency where the center of the phase transition occurs.	Controls how sharp the transition is at the selected frequency. The larger this value, the sharper the transition produced.	*Not used*

▌ Creating an Equalizer

Two of the most common types of equalizers are parametric and graphic. A graphic equalizer allows you to boost or attenuate a series of *fixed* frequencies but does not include the ability to modify the bandwidth of those selected frequencies. Parametric equalizers, on the contrary, allow you to select a specific frequency, boost or attenuate it, and change the bandwidth range. You can use BiquadFilter nodes to design either of these equalizers, and many others.

▌ Graphic EQ

The following diagram and code show how to create a seven-band graphic equalizer. You do this by chaining a series of BiquadFilter nodes together and setting their type properties to peaking. Keep in mind that the only parameter the user of a graphic equalizer should be allowed to change is the gain of each filter. The input and output source for this example is abstracted using a function named multibandEQ.

16. The Biquad Filter Node

```
let filter1 = audioContext.createBiquadFilter();
filter1.type = "peaking"; /*_____Do not let user modify. This is a
    graphic EQ!*/
filter1.gain.value = 0;
filter1.Q.value = 1; /*_____Do not let user modify. This is a
    graphic EQ!*/
filter1.frequency.value = 64; /*_Do not let user modify. This is a
    graphic EQ!*/
let filter2 = audioContext.createBiquadFilter();
filter2.type = "peaking"; /*_____Do not let user modify. This is a
    graphic EQ!*/
filter2.gain.value = 0;
filter2.Q.value = 1; /*_____Do not let user modify. This is a
    graphic EQ!*/
filter2.frequency.value = 150; /*_Do not let user modify. This is a
    graphic EQ!*/
let filter3 = audioContext.createBiquadFilter();
filter3.type = "peaking"; /*_____Do not let user modify. This is a
    graphic EQ!*/
filter3.gain.value = 0;
filter3.Q.value = 1; /*_____Do not let user modify. This is a
    graphic EQ!*/
filter3.frequency.value = 350; /*_Do not let user modify. This is a
    graphic EQ!*/
let filter4 = audioContext.createBiquadFilter();
filter4.type = "peaking"; /*_____Do not let user modify. This is a
    graphic EQ!*/
filter4.gain.value = 0;
filter4.Q.value = 1; /*_____Do not let user modify. This is a
    graphic EQ!*/
filter4.frequency.value = 1000; /*Do not let user modify. This is a
    graphic EQ!*/
let filter5 = audioContext.createBiquadFilter();
filter5.type = "peaking"; /*_____Do not let user modify. This is a
    graphic EQ!*/
filter5.gain.value = 0;
filter5.Q.value = 1; /*_____Do not let user modify. This is a
    graphic EQ!*/
filter5.frequency.value = 2000; /*Do not let user modify. This is a
    graphic EQ!*/
let filter6 = audioContext.createBiquadFilter();
filter6.type = "peaking"; /*_____Do not let user modify. This is a
    graphic EQ!*/
filter6.gain.value = 0;
filter6.Q.value = 1; /*_____Do not let user modify. This is a
    graphic EQ!*/
filter6.frequency.value = 6000; /*Do not let user modify. This is a
    graphic EQ!*/
let filter7 = audioContext.createBiquadFilter();
filter7.type = "peaking"; /*_____Do not let user modify. This is a
    graphic EQ!*/
filter7.gain.value = 0;
filter7.Q.value = 1; /*_____Do not let user modify. This is a
    graphic EQ!*/
filter7.frequency.value = 12000; /*Do not let user modify. This is a
    graphic EQ!*/
function multibandEQ(inputConnection, outputConnection)
{
```

```
inputConnection.connect(filter1);
filter1.connect(filter2);
filter2.connect(filter3);
filter3.connect(filter4);
filter4.connect(filter5);
filter5.connect(filter6);
filter6.connect(filter7);
filter7.connect(outputConnection);
}
```

The code files for this chapter include versions of both the graphic and parametric equalizers with user interface controls. These applications allow you to toggle the playback of a song and change parameters of the BiquadFilter nodes in real time by using the interactive sliders.

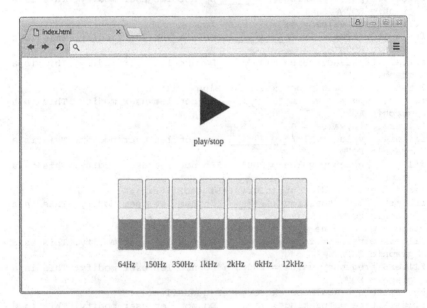

▮ Parametric EQ

You can design a parametric equalizer in a similar way to the graphic equalizer by chaining a series of BiquadFilter nodes together and setting their type properties to peaking. The primary difference of the parametric equalizer is that the frequency, gain, and bandwidth are modifiable by the user. Keep in mind that with multiband parametric equalizers, the filter type may have multiple options available. To keep the code simple and short, the following example shows how to create a *single*-band parametric equalizer with type set to the value peaking. The input and output source in this code is abstracted using a function named parametricEQ.

```
let parametricEQ1 = audioContext.createBiquadFilter();
parametricEQ1.type = "peaking";
parametricEQ1.gain.value = 0; // allow the user to change this
parametricEQ1.Q.value = 1; // allow the user to change this
parametricEQ1.frequency.value = 1000;
function parametricEQ(inputConnection, outputConnection) {
  inputConnection.connect(parametricEQ1);
  parametricEQ1.connect(outputConnection);
}
```

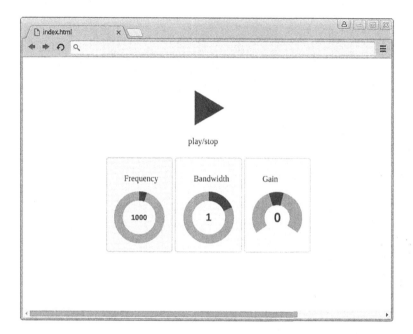

▌ Summary

In this chapter, you learned about the BiquadFilter node and how to use it to create custom equalizers and filter arrangements. Keep in mind that the examples here are kept simple, and like the node graph itself, your filter arrangements can be as complex as you want to make them. In the next chapter, you will learn about another signal processing node: the convolver node.

17 The Convolver Node

In this chapter, you will learn how to use the convolver node. The convolver allows you to apply reverberation to node graph input sources by referencing a special kind of audio file called an impulse response.

▌ Convolution Reverb

When an acoustic sound is created, its characteristics are shaped by its immediate environment. This is due to sound waves bouncing off and around various obstacles. These obstacles can be made of different materials that affect the sound in different ways. The result of sound emanating from a small room has different characteristics than sound emanating from a large room. Because the human ear can hear these differences, when this information is transmitted to the brain, we perceive these characteristics as room *ambience*. Modern advancements in digital audio technology allow us to record the ambience of any real-world environment and apply it to any digital audio signal directly. These *recorded ambiences* are stored as a special file called an impulse response. An impulse response file is made by recording a single sound burst in an environment, which could be white noise, a sine wave sweep, or even a balloon pop. This recording is then run through a special digital algorithm to create a single file called an impulse response. This impulse response file is combined *or convolved* with another input

DOI: 10.1201/9781003201496-17

source to give the targeted sound the spacial characteristics of the room that the impulse is modeled from.

The format of impulse response files can be any audio file type including WAV, MP3, AIFF, or OGG. However, to use them with the Web Audio API, impulse response files must be in a browser-compatible audio format. For this chapter, we use WAV files because they are of higher quality than MP3 files. And because impulse response files are small, load time is not a concern.

■ Where to Get Pre-Recorded Impulse Response Files

There are many online resources where you can download impulse response files for free, such as: http://www.openairlib.net/.

■ Using Impulse Response Files

To use impulse response files, you must first load them, decode them, and store them in a buffer.

```
const audioContext = new AudioContext();
let impulseResponseBuffer;
let getSound = new XMLHttpRequest();
getSound.open("get", "sounds/impulse.wav", true); // impulse file
getSound.responseType = "arraybuffer";
getSound.onload = function() {
 audioContext.decodeAudioData(getSound.response, function(buffer) {
    impulseResponseBuffer = buffer;
  });
};
getSound.send();
```

After the file is stored in a buffer, the next step is to wire up the necessary nodes to apply the effect to an input source. To integrate the impulse response into the node graph configuration, you must first create a convolver node using audioContext.createConvolver() and store the returned object in a variable.

```
let convolver = audioContext.createConvolver();
```

You then assign the loaded impulse response buffer to the buffer property of the object.

```
convolver.buffer = impulseResponseBuffer;
```

Next, you connect any input source you want to the convolver node. Here is an example of connecting an oscillator.

The following HTML and JavaScript code combine the impulse file loader, node graph connections, and JQuery DOM selectors to allow you to play the oscillator by clicking an HTML button and holding it. This allows you to hear the reverberation effect more explicitly because the reverb tail is audible after removing your finger from the mouse button and stopping the oscillator.

▌ HTML

```
<!DOCTYPE html>
<html>
  <head>
    <meta charset="UTF-8">
    <title></title>
    <script type="text/javascript" src="https://ajax.googleapis.
      com/ajax/libs/jquery/3.6.0/jquery.min.js "></script>
    <script src="js/app.js"></script>
  </head>
  <body>
    <button>Oscillation</button>
  </body>
</html>
```

▌ JavaScript

```
"use strict";
const audioContext = new AudioContext();
let impulseResponseBuffer;
let getSound = new XMLHttpRequest();
getSound.open("get", "sounds/impulse.wav", true);
getSound.responseType = "arraybuffer";
getSound.onload = function() {
 audioContext.decodeAudioData(getSound.response, function(buffer) {
    impulseResponseBuffer = buffer;
  });
};
getSound.send();


/*_____BEGIN playback
   functionality*/
let osc = audioContext.createOscillator();
function playback() {
  let  convolver = audioContext.createConvolver();
  osc = audioContext.createOscillator();
  osc.type = "sawtooth";
  convolver.buffer = impulseResponseBuffer;
  osc.connect(convolver);
  convolver.connect(audioContext.destination);
  osc.start(audioContext.currentTime);
}
$(function() {
  $("button").on("mousedown", function() {
    playback();
  });
  $("button").on("mouseup", function() {
    osc.stop();
```

```
    });
});
```

▌ Controlling the Amount of Reverberation

In the previous code example, the amount of reverb applied to the oscillator is fixed at 100 percent. If you want to make the effect variable, which allows you to control how much of the effect is applied to the input source, you can do so by splitting the input source with a gain node and routing one split to the convolver node prior to connecting it to the destination. You then connect the other split directly to the destination. You use gain.value to blend the amount of the effect you want to hear.

The following diagram and node graph configuration code demonstrate the splitting operation.

```
let gain = audioContext.createGain();
let convolver = audioContext.createConvolver();
osc = audioContext.createOscillator();
osc.type = "sawtooth";
convolver.buffer = impulseResponseBuffer;
osc.connect(convolver);
convolver.connect(gain);
gain.gain.value = 0.2;
gain.connect(audioContext.destination);
osc.connect(audioContext.destination);
osc.start(audioContext.currentTime);
```

▌ Summary

In this chapter, you learned how to use the convolver node to apply an impulse response file to an input source. You also learned how to use gain nodes to control the amount of the effect you want to hear. In the next chapter, you will learn how to modify the panning of stereo input sources and how to create sophisticated routing schemes using the channel and merger nodes.

18 Stereo Panning, Channel Splitting, and Merging

The Web Audio API includes a stereo panner node that lets you pan input sources to any part of the stereo field. It also includes nodes that let you split multichannel audio files into separate channels as well as merge multichannel input sources into a specified output channel. In this chapter, you will learn how to use these nodes to manipulate multichannel input sources.

◼ The Stereo Panner Node

To use the stereo panner node, you first invoke `createStereoPanner()` and store the returned object in a variable.

```
let stereoPanner = audioContext.createStereoPanner();
```

You can then connect any input source to the node and use `pan.value` to set the location in the stereo field where you want to place the sound. The `pan.value` property setting is a number between 1 and −1, where 1 represents a 100 percent pan to the right and −1 represents a 100 percent pan to the left. In the following example, an oscillator is connected to a stereo panner node and is set 50 percent to the left.

```
let oscillator = audioContext.createOscillator();
let stereoPanner = audioContext.createStereoPanner();
```

DOI: 10.1201/9781003201496-18

```
stereoPanner.pan.value = -0.5;
oscillator.connect(stereoPanner);
stereoPanner.connect(audioContext.destination);
oscillator.start(audioContext.currentTime);
```

The stereoPanner() uses an equal power algorithm to pan input sources. This means that when a stereo input source is panned, the audio content on the attenuated side is *summed* with the audio on the amplified side.

▋ The Channel Splitter

If you want to isolate the individual channels of a multichannel input source or do not want your stereo input sources to be subjected to an equal power algorithm, you must use the channel splitter. This node isolates any channel of a multichannel input source for further processing. This applies to both stereo and other multichannel audio input sources, such as 5.1 surround files. To create a channel splitter, you invoke the createChannelSplitter() method with a single argument and store the returned object in a variable. The argument value is the number of channels of the audio source material that you intend to connect to the splitter. If no argument is specified, the default is 6. In the following example, a stereo file is split, so the argument is set to 2.

```
let splitter = audioContext.createChannelSplitter(2);
```

To use the channel splitter, you connect input sources to it and then connect the splitter to other nodes. When connecting the splitter to a destination node, you specify the channel of the input source to connect to in the second argument of the connect() method. This argument is a number that represents the channel as an index value. The following chart displays the index for each channel of a six-channel input source.

Channel	Index Value
L	0
R	1
SL	2
SR	3
C	4
LFE	5

The following code shows the correspondence between the channel index argument and its respective channel type:

```
stereoInputSource.connect(splitter);
splitter.connect(audioContext.destination, 0); /*outputs left
   side/channel of stereo input source*/
splitter.connect(audioContext.destination, 1); /*outputs right
   side/channel of stereo input source*/
```

The following code shows how to modify the gain value of individual left and right channels of a stereo input source. In other words, this configuration is the opposite of an equal power panning algorithm.

```
let splitter = audioContext.createChannelSplitter(2);
let pannerLeft = audioContext.createStereoPanner();
let pannerRight = audioContext.createStereoPanner();
let left = audioContext.createGain();
let right = audioContext.createGain();
let sound = audioContext.createBufferSource();
sound.loop = true;
sound.buffer = bufferSource;
sound.connect(splitter);
splitter.connect(left, 0); //___connect left channel to gain node
splitter.connect(right, 1); //__connect right channel to gain node
left.gain.value = leftVal; /*_____independent left channel
    control*/
right.gain.value = rightVal; /*_____independent right channel
    control*/
left.connect(pannerLeft);
pannerLeft.pan.value = -1;
pannerRight.pan.value = 1;
right.connect(pannerRight);
pannerLeft.connect(audioContext.destination);
pannerRight.connect(audioContext.destination);
sound.start(audioContext.currentTime + time || audioContext.
    currentTime);
```

▌ The Channel Merger

If you want to combine multiple mono input sources and route them to a specific channel in the stereo (or multichannel) spectrum, you use a channel merger. The function invocation for the channel merger node takes one argument that determines how many input channels the object accepts. If no argument is given, the default is 6.

```
let merger = audioContext.createChannelMerger();
```

When connecting an input source to a channel merger, you must specify the output channel using the third argument of the connect method.

```
inputSource.connect(merger, 0, 1); /*outputs all channels of
    inputSource to right channel*/
```

▌ Merging All Channels of a Multichannel File into a Single Mono Channel

To combine a multichannel file into a single *mono* output, which is placed at the center of the stereo spectrum, you set the channel merger invocation argument to 1, and then connect the input source to the channel merger.

```
let multiChannelInputSource = audioContext.createBufferSource();
let merger = audioContext.createChannelMerger(1); /*Set number of
    channels*/
stereoInputSource.buffer = audioBuffer;
stereoInputSource.connect(merger);
merger.connect(audioContext.destination);
```

■ Using the Merger and Splitter Nodes Together

The merger and splitter nodes can be used in conjunction with one another to route specific input channels to specific output channels. The following code takes the left and right sides of a stereo input source and swaps them.

```
stereoInputSource.connect(splitter);
splitter.connect(merger, 0, 1); // input left and output right
splitter.connect(merger, 1, 0); // input right and output left
merger.connect(audioContext.destination);
```

If you connect an audio input source, such as an audio buffer source node, directly to a channel merger node, there is no reason to set the second argument of the connect method to a value other than 0. This is because the merger node has a *single* output.

```
audioBufferSource.connect(merger, 0, 1);
```

If the input of a channel merger is a channel splitter, the second argument of the connect method is the channel of the input source sent to the merger.

```
let channelSplitter = audioContext.createChannelSplitter();
let channelMerger = audioContext.createChannelMerger();
let sound = audioContext.createBufferSource();
sound.buffer = audioBuffer;
sound.connect(channelSplitter);
channelSplitter.connect(channelMerger, 0, 0); /*The left channel
    of playSound is connected to the channel merger*/
channelMerger.connect(audioContext.destination);
```

■ Summary

In this chapter, you learned how to apply stereo panning to audio input sources. You also learned how to work with the channel splitter and channel merger nodes. In the next chapter, you will explore how to create delay effects using the delay node.

19 The Delay Node

In the world of creative audio, delays are a common method used to create time-based effects. In this chapter, you will learn how to use the delay node to create the most common delay effects: echo, slap back, and ping-pong.

▮▮ The Delay Node

The delay node is used to adjust the time between when an input source plays and when it becomes audible. The following example connects an audio buffer to a delay node. The delayTime.value property determines the delay time in seconds.

```
let sound = audioContext.createBufferSource();
let delay = audioContext.createDelay();
delay.delayTime.value = 1; // One second
sound.buffer = audioBuffer;
sound.connect(delay);
delay.connect(audioContext.destination);
sound.start(audioContext.currentTime);
```

If you listen to the result of the previous example, you will notice that it does not provide the repetitive echo delay effect that is typical of an effects processor. This is because the only thing the delay node does is pause the audio from playing for a set amount of time. If you want a repetitive echo effect, you must create it.

▌▌ Creating Echo Effects

To create an echo effect, you configure a node graph scheme that sets the delayed signal to feed back on itself.

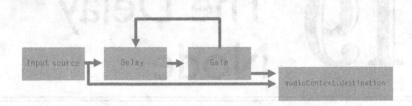

The `gain.value` property controls the amount of the effect and the `delayTime.value` property controls the length of the delay. The following code applies the effect to an audio buffer.

```
let sound = audioContext.createBufferSource();
let delayAmount = audioContext.createGain();
let delay = audioContext.createDelay();
sound.buffer = audioBuffer;
delay.delayTime.value = 0.5;
delayAmount.gain.value = 0.5;
sound.connect(delay);
delay.connect(delayAmount);
delayAmount.connect(delay);
delayAmount.connect(audioContext.destination);
sound.connect(audioContext.destination);
sound.start(audioContext.currentTime);
```

▌▌ Creating Slap Back Effects

A slap back effect is a quick delay of 40–140 milliseconds. To create this type of effect, you split an input source and connect one branch to the delay and the other branch to the destination. You also connect the delay node to a gain node to control the volume of the effect. The node configuration for a slap back is shown in the following example and figure.

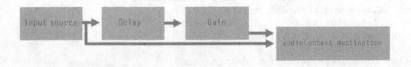

```
let sound = audioContext.createBufferSource();
let delayAmount = audioContext.createGain();
let delay = audioContext.createDelay();
sound.buffer = audioBuffer;
delay.delayTime.value = 0.06;
delayAmount.gain.value = 0.5;
```

```
sound.connect(delay);
delay.connect(delayAmount);
delayAmount.connect(audioContext.destination);
sound.connect(audioContext.destination);
sound.start(audioContext.currentTime);
```

■ Creating a Ping-Pong Delay

A ping-pong effect is an echo delay where the echo toggles between the left and right sides of the stereo spectrum. This effect can be created by spitting an input source to the left and right outputs, running each of those outputs through independent delay and gain nodes, and then feeding back the signal from the gain to its own delay as well as the delay being used to process the other side of the stereo spectrum.

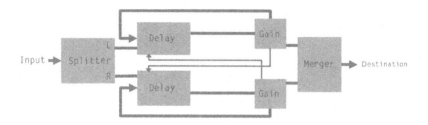

The following code implements the configuration shown in the above figure:

```
//_____BEGIN setup
let sound = audioContext.createBufferSource();
sound.buffer = audioBuffer;
let merger = audioContext.createChannelMerger(2);
let splitter = audioContext.createChannelSplitter(2);
let leftDelay = audioContext.createDelay();
let rightDelay = audioContext.createDelay();
let leftFeedback = audioContext.createGain();
let rightFeedback = audioContext.createGain();

//_____END setup
sound.connect(splitter);
sound.connect(audioContext.destination);
splitter.connect(leftDelay, 0);
leftDelay.delayTime.value = 0.5;
leftDelay.connect(leftFeedback);
leftFeedback.gain.value = 0.6;
leftFeedback.connect(rightDelay);
splitter.connect(rightDelay, 1);
rightDelay.delayTime.value = 0.5;
rightFeedback.gain.value = 0.6;
rightDelay.connect(rightFeedback);
rightFeedback.connect(leftDelay);
leftFeedback.connect(merger, 0, 0);
rightFeedback.connect(merger, 0, 1);
```

```
//_____BEGIN output
merger.connect(audioContext.destination);

//_____END output
sound.start(audioContext.currentTime);
```

▌ Summary

The delay node by itself is not complicated or difficult to use, but when combined with other nodes it can be a powerful tool for the creation of interesting audio effects. In the next chapter, you will continue exploring the node graph and learn how to apply dynamic range compression to audio input sources.

20 Dynamic Range Compression

In this chapter, you will learn about the dynamics compressor node. This node allows you to apply dynamic range compression to audio input sources.

▪ The Dynamics Compressor Node

Dynamic range compression is the process of automatically attenuating an audio signal when its decibel level exceeds a specified threshold. This is analogous to manually turning down the volume knob on your radio when a piece of music gets too loud and then turning it back up during a quieter passage. When this action is done with a dynamic range compressor, you get the benefits of automation, speed, and the precision of a computer.

The Web Audio API comes with a built-in tool called the dynamics compressor node that allows you to apply dynamic range compression to audio input sources. To use it, you must first invoke the `createDynamicsCompressor()` method and store the resulting object in a variable.

```
let compressor = audioContext.createDynamicsCompressor();
```

The object provides you with a collection of five properties that affect the dynamic range of an audio input source. A sixth property called `reduction` is also available, but it does not affect the input source in any way. The reduction property is used exclusively to output a reduction value. These properties are briefly described in the following chart. All properties except `reduction` take a number as their assignment. The `reduction` property provides only a readout value.

Property	Description
Threshold	The decibel value above which the compression will start taking effect. Its default value is −24, with a nominal range of −100 to 0
Ratio	Determines how much compression is administered. Setting the ratio to 2 means that for every 2 dB that the signal exceeds the threshold there will be only 1 dB in amplitude change. The ratio property takes a number between 1 and 20
Knee	A decibel value representing the range above the threshold where a curve is created that smoothly transitions to the compressed part of the signal. Its default value is 30, with a nominal range of 0–40
Release	Sets the release speed of the compression effect. The amount of time (in seconds) to reduce the gain by 10 dB. Its default value is 0.003, with a nominal range of 0–1
Attack	Sets the attack speed of the compression effect. The amount of time (in seconds) to increase the gain by 10 dB. Its default value is 0.250, with a nominal range of 0 to 1
Reduction	A numeric readout of the reduction being applied. The reduction property does not affect the signal and is used for metering purposes

The following code demonstrates how to apply the dynamics compressor node to an audio input source. In this example, for every 12 dB the signal surpasses a threshold of −40 dB, its output is increased by 1 dB.

```
//_____BEGIN setup
  let sound = audioContext.createBufferSource();
  let compressor = audioContext.createDynamicsCompressor();
  sound.buffer = audioBuffer;

//_____END setup
  sound.connect(compressor);
  compressor.threshold.value = -40;
  compressor.ratio.value = 12;

//_____BEGIN output
  compressor.connect(audioContext.destination);

//_____END output
  sound.start(audioContext.currentTime);
```

Anyone familiar with the world of creative audio will immediately be familiar with every property available to the dynamics compressor node *except one*: `reduction`. The `reduction` property, specific to the Web Audio API, outputs a numeric value representing the amount of reduction the compressor is imposing on the input source. The following code uses `setInterval()` to allow you to see the change in reduction value as an audio input source is compressed.

```
//_____BEGIN setup
let compressor = audioContext.createDynamicsCompressor();
let sound = audioContext.createBufferSource();
sound.buffer = audioBuffer;

//_____END setup
sound.connect(compressor);
compressor.threshold.value = -40;
compressor.ratio.value = 12;

   //_____BEGIN output
compressor.connect(audioContext.destination);

   //_____END output
sound.start(audioContext.currentTime);
window.setInterval(function() {
   console.log(compressor.reduction);
}, 50);
```

◼ Summary

Using the dynamics compressor node is not complicated. It contains all the basic parameters needed to modify the dynamic range of any input source connected to it.

In the next chapter, you will learn how to work with time in the Web Audio API.

21 Time

In this chapter, you will learn how to work with time to schedule Web Audio API sound playback points, how to create loops, and how to automate parameter changes.

▌ The Timing Clock

When you invoke a new instance of the audio context, the Web Audio API's internal timing clock begins to tick. This timing reference is in *seconds* and is expressed as a decimal number. The timing clock is tied to your computer's internal audio hardware subsystem, giving it a degree of precision that can align with sounds at the sample level. If you want to see the current value of the audio clock, you can use the currentTime property of the audio context.

```
console.log(audioContext.currentTime);
```

When you play an audio event, the Web Audio API requires you to *schedule* it. Remember that the unit you use for time value scheduling is *seconds*. If you want to schedule an event immediately, you can use the currentTime property of the audio context.

You have already had some exposure to scheduling the playback of sounds in previous chapters, such as in the following example code:

```
sound.start(audioContext.currentTime); // Play immediately
sound.start(audioContext.currentTime + 2); /*Play audio buffer two
    seconds into the future*/
```

■ The start Method

The start method is used to begin a sound playing. The start method takes three arguments. The first argument schedules when the sound plays, either immediately or in the future. The second argument sets a start point that determines where to begin playback from in the audio buffer. The third argument sets when a sound ceases to play. For a real-world example, imagine you were playing back a 4/4 drum loop and 0.5 seconds into the loop the drummer hit the snare drum. If you want to start playback from this point, you set the second argument of start() to 0.5.

```
sound.start(audioContext.currentTime,0.5);
```

The third argument sets how much of the sound will play. If you have a sound that is 4 seconds long and you only want to hear the first 2 seconds, then you set the third argument to 2.

```
sound.start(audioContext.currentTime,0, 2);
```

■ Looping Sounds

To loop sounds, you set the loop property of an audio buffer source node to true. To set the start point of a loop, you use the property loopStart. To set the end point of a loop, you use the property loopEnd.

```
sound.loop = true;
    sound.loopStart = 1; /*Set loop point at one second after
        beginning of playback*/
    sound.loopEnd = 2; /*Set loop end point at two seconds after
        beginning of playback*/
```

Sometimes when trying to discern playback and loop points, it is useful to know the length of an audio file. You can get this information using a property of the sound buffer named duration.

```
let sound = audioContext.createBufferSource();
sound.buffer = buffer;
sound.buffer.duration; // length in seconds of audio file
```

Included in the code examples for this chapter is an application that allows you to modify the playback and loop points of an audio file in real-time using interactive sliders.

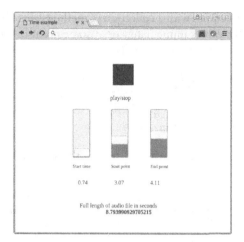

▉ Update Your Audio Loader Library

The play() method of your audio loader library is not designed to access the second and third arguments of the start method. You can make these arguments available with the following modifications to your code:

```
soundObj.play = function(time, setStart, setDuration) {
  playSound = audioContext.createBufferSource();

  playSound.buffer = soundObj.soundToPlay;
  playSound.start(audioContext.currentTime + time || audioContext.
    currentTime, setStart || 0, setDuration || soundObj.
soundToPlay.
      duration);

    if (nodeGraph) {
         return nodeGraph(playSound);
       } else {
         return playSound.connect(audioContext.destination);
       }
};
```

The start and end point settings are now available.

```
sounds.snare.play(0, 0.5, 3);
```

▉ Changing Audio Parameters over Time

Up to this point you have changed audio parameters by directly setting the value property to a number.

```
let osc = audioContext.createOscillator();
osc.frequency.value = 300;
```

The Web Audio API comes with a collection of methods that allow you to schedule audio parameter values immediately or at some point in the future. The following code shows a list of these methods.

```
setValueAtTime(arg1,arg2)
exponentialRampToValueAtTime(arg1,arg2)
linearRampToValueAtTime(arg1,arg2)
setTargetAtTime(arg1,arg2,arg3)
setValueCurveAtTime(arg1,arg2,arg3)
```

You can use these methods in place of setting the value property of an audio parameter.

```
osc.frequency.value = 100; // Set value directly
osc.frequency.setValueAtTime(arg1,arg2); /*Set value with audio
  parameter method*/
```

▌ The Audio Parameter Methods

The setValueAtTime Method

The setValueAtTime method allows you to create an abrupt change of an audio parameter at a future period in time. The first argument is the value the parameter will be changed to, and the second argument is the time that it will take to change to that value. In the following example, 5 seconds after the code is run, a gain node parameter value is abruptly changed from 1 to 0.1.

```
let osc = audioContext.createOscillator();
let volume = audioContext.createGain();
osc.connect(volume);
volume.gain.value = 1;
volume.gain.setValueAtTime(0.1,audioContext.currentTime + 5);
osc.start(audioContext.currentTime);
volume.connect(audioContext.destination);
```

To use any of the other audio parameter methods that are described next, you must first initialize their settings using setValueAtTime(). This is shown in the code examples for each method.

The exponentialRampToValueAtTime Method

The exponentialRampToValueAtTime() method allows you to create a gradual change of the parameter value. Unlike the abrupt change of setValueAtTime(), this method follows an exponential curve. The following code demonstrates this by changing an oscillator's frequency from 200 Hz to 3 kHz over the course of 3 seconds.

```
let osc = audioContext.createOscillator();
let volume = audioContext.createGain();
```

```
osc.frequency.value = 200;
osc.frequency.setValueAtTime(osc.frequency.value, audioContext.
  currentTime); //___Set initial values!
osc.frequency.exponentialRampToValueAtTime(3000, audioContext.
  currentTime + 3);
osc.start(audioContext.currentTime);
osc.connect(audioContext.destination);
```

The linearRampToValueAtTime Method

The linearRampToValueAtTime method is similar to exponential-RampToValueAtTime() but follows a gradual *linear* curve instead of an exponential curve.

```
let osc = audioContext.createOscillator();
let volume = audioContext.createGain();
osc.frequency.value = 200;
osc.frequency.setValueAtTime(osc.frequency.value, audioContext.
  currentTime); // Set initial values
osc.frequency.linearRampToValueAtTime(3000, audioContext.
  currentTime + 3);
osc.start(audioContext.currentTime);
osc.connect(audioContext.destination);
```

The setTargetAtTime() Method

The setTargetAtTime() method takes three arguments. The first argument is the *final* value of the audio parameter, the second argument is the time the change will *begin*, and the third argument is a time constant that determines *how long* the change will take to complete. The larger the number of the third argument, the longer the change takes to complete.

```
let osc = audioContext.createOscillator();
let volume = audioContext.createGain();
osc.frequency.value = 200;
osc.frequency.setValueAtTime(osc.frequency.value, audioContext.
  currentTime); // Set initial values
osc.frequency.setTargetAtTime(3000, audioContext.currentTime,2);
osc.start(audioContext.currentTime);
osc.connect(audioContext.destination);
```

The setValueCurveAtTime() Method

The setValueCurveAtTime() method allows you to create a custom curve based on a collection of audio parameter values stored in an array. This method takes three arguments. The first argument is an array of values. The array used is a special kind of array called a float32Array(), which is a *typed* array. Typed arrays are better performing than conventional arrays and allow some Web Audio APIs to work directly with binary data. The syntax for a float32Array()

requires you to explicitly set the number of index values and looks like the following code:

```
let waveArray = new Float32Array(10); //__Set number of index
values
waveArray[0] = 20;
waveArray[1] = 200;
waveArray[2] = 20;
waveArray[3] = 200;
waveArray[4] = 20;
waveArray[5] = 200;
waveArray[6] = 20;
waveArray[7] = 200;
waveArray[8] = 20;
waveArray[9] = 200;
```

The second argument represents when you want the changes to begin, and the third argument is the time span you want the changes to take place within. The following code demonstrates this by toggling the frequency of an oscillator from 100 to 500 Hz and back again over the course of 3 seconds. This creates a *wobble* effect.

```
let waveArray = new Float32Array(10);
waveArray[0] = 100;
waveArray[1] = 500;
waveArray[2] = 100;
waveArray[3] = 500;
waveArray[4] = 100;
waveArray[5] = 500;
waveArray[6] = 100;
waveArray[7] = 500;
waveArray[8] = 100;
waveArray[9] = 500;
let osc = audioContext.createOscillator();
let volume = audioContext.createGain();
osc.frequency.value = 500;
osc.frequency.setValueAtTime(osc.frequency.value, audioContext.
  currentTime); // Set initial values
osc.frequency.setValueCurveAtTime(waveArray, audioContext.
  currentTime + 1, 3);
osc.start(audioContext.currentTime);
osc.connect(audioContext.destination);
```

▍ Summary

In this chapter, you learned the fundamentals of working with time. You learned how to loop and schedule sound playback, as well as how to schedule parameter value changes. In the next chapter, you will learn how to create audio visualizations using the Analyser node.

22 Creating Audio Visualizations

In this chapter, you will learn how to use the `Analyser` node to create a spectrum analyzer that displays real-time amplitude information of audio signals across a collection of frequency bands. The Web Audio API includes a node named `Analyser` that gives you real-time frequency and time domain information about audio input sources. This information can be used to create custom visual representations of audio signals that include (but are not limited to) spectrum analyzers, phase scopes, and waveform renders.

▌ A Brief Word on Fourier Analysis

Before you get started, you must first have a basic conceptual understanding of Fourier analysis. Fourier analysis is a difficult topic involving a lot of impressive math, so a proper coverage of the topic is *well* beyond the scope of this book. The main point you need to understand is that Fourier analysis is a way to take amazingly complex things like sound waves and simplify them. With this approach, a signal (referred to as a function) can be either represented or approximated by a combination of simpler periodic signals or functions, such as sine and cosine waves. Replicating a sound is also theoretically possible by *combining* an infinite number of these waveforms. In theory, a perfect replica (or perfect separation of constituent parts) is realized from this combination, but in practice, human beings lack infinite time and computing power, so you will always have to make do with an approximation.

Some of the most common forms of Fourier analysis in audio processing are called *fast Fourier transforms*, or more commonly FFTs. The goal of an FFT is to quickly give you a useful approximation without doing too much computational work and slowing down the system.

▌ A Brief Explanation of Binary-Coded Decimal Numbers

To better understand how the Web Audio API gives you access to the time and frequency domain of audio input sources, you need to understand how to read binary-coded decimal numbers. A binary system is composed of a series of *on* and *off* values called bits. Bits are read in 8-bit groupings called bytes, which have an equivalent decimal value. Bits are read from right to left and each value is either an *on* value represented by a 1, or an *off* value represented by a 0. The decimal equivalent of a grouping of bits is calculated by exponentially counting from right to left and adding all of the *on* values together.

```
Byte:      00001001
                ↓    ↓
Decimal:       8 + 1 = 9
```

When all bits are *on*, a byte has a value of 255. This allows for 256 total possible values (0–255).

$$1\ 1\ 1\ 1\ 1\ 1\ 1\ 1$$

128 + 64 + 32 + 16 + 8 + 4 + 2 + 1

Total: 255

(256 possible decimal values)

▌ The Spectrum Analyzer

The following program creates a basic frequency spectrum analyzer using an oscillator as its input source. The rest of this chapter is dedicated to explaining how this code works.

▌ JavaScript/JQuery

```javascript
"use strict";
$(function() {
  let audioContext = new AudioContext();
  let analyzer = audioContext.createAnalyser();
  let osc = audioContext.createOscillator();
  let frequencyData = new Uint8Array(analyzer.frequencyBinCount);
    //___Create array
  analyzer.getByteFrequencyData(frequencyData);
    //_____Store frequency data
  console.log(frequencyData.length);
  console.log(frequencyData);
  let app = $(".app");
  let bars = undefined;
  osc.frequency.value = 120;
  osc.connect(analyzer);
  analyzer.connect(audioContext.destination);
  osc.start(audioContext.currentTime);
  analyzer.fftSize = 2048;
  console.log(analyzer.frequencyBinCount); // 1024
  //_____BEGIN Visualization
  $(".bin-count-number").text(analyzer.fftSize / 2); //____Bin
count
  for (let i = 0; i < analyzer.frequencyBinCount; i++) {
    $(".app").append("<div></div> <span>" + i + "</span>");
  }
  bars = $(".app > div");
  function update() {
    requestAnimationFrame(update);
    analyzer.getByteFrequencyData(frequencyData);
    for (let i = 0; i < bars.length; i += 1) {
      bars[i].style.height = frequencyData[i] + 'px';
    }
  }
  update();
  //_____END visualization
});
```

▌ HTML

```html
<!DOCTYPE html>
<html>
  <head>
    <meta charset="UTF-8">
    <title></title>
    <script type="text/javascript" src="js/jquery.js"></script>
    <script src="js/app.js"></script>
    <link rel="stylesheet" href="css/app.css" type="text/css">
  </head>
  <!--_____BEGIN
```

```
    APP-->
  <body>
    <p class="bin-count">
      Bin count:<b class="bin-count-number"></b>
    </p>
    <div class="app">
    </div>
  </body>
  <!--_____END
    APP-->
</html>
```

▊ CSS

```
.app{
  position: relative;
  margin: 10px;
}
.app > div {
  width: 0.1px;
  background-color: orange;
  display: inline-block;
  outline-style:solid;
  outline-color:orange;
  outline-width: 0.1px;
  margin-left:8px;
}
span{
  display:inline-block;
  font-size:14px;
  color:rgba(128, 128, 128, 0.5);
  margin:2px;
}
.bin-count{
  position:absolute;
  left:30%;
  float:right;
  font-size:2em;
  height:50px;
}
```

The output of the application looks like the following figure.

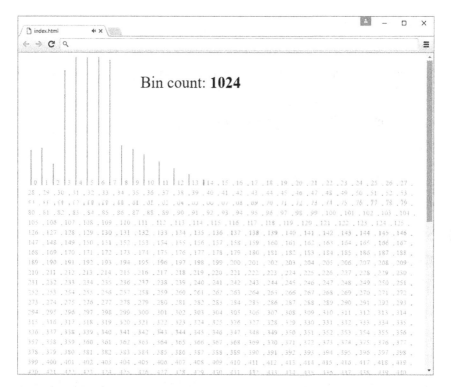

■ Walking through the Code

The first step to creating a spectrum analyzer is to invoke `Analyser()` and connect input sources to the returned object. For this application, the only input source used is an `oscillator` and the output of the `analyser` variable is connected directly to `audioContext.destination`.

```
let analyzer = audioContext.createAnalyser();
let oscillator = audioContext.createOscillator();
oscillator.connect(analyzer);
analyzer.connect(audioContext.destination);
```

The `Analyser` interface enables you to perform various FFTs on the audio stream. The FFT used to create a spectrum analyzer transforms the time domain of the audio signal into normalized (or limited) frequency-domain data. This is done by chopping the original audio signal into parts, typically called *bins*, and performing an analysis and transformation on each part.

The size of the FFT is stored in the `fftSize` property of the `Analyser` node and the default value is 2048. The allowed values are any power of 2 between 32 and 2048. If you set it wrong, you will get an error. The number of bins available is one half of the `fftSize` property and is accessible by a read-only property of the `Analyser` node named `frequencyBinCount`.

```
analyzer.fftSize = 2048;
console.log(analyzer.frequencyBinCount); // 1024... or half of
fftSize
```

Each bin is designated a range of frequencies called a *band*, and the following formula determines the range of each band:

(Sample Rate)/(FFT Size)=(Band Size)

Example:

44,100/2048=21.533203125

▮ Storing the Frequency Data in an Array

The next step is to create an array to store the frequency data. A special kind of array called a *typed* array is required for this task. A typed array is an array-like object specifically designed for working with binary data.

```
//_____Create typed array
let frequencyData = new Uint8Array(analyzer.frequencyBinCount);
//_____Store frequency data
analyzer.getByteFrequencyData(frequencyData);
```

There are two kinds of typed arrays that the Analyser node is designed to work with: Float32Array and Uint8Array. The index values of a Float32Array are always a decimal number between 0 and 1. The index values of a Uint8Array are limited to 8 bits of information and will always be an integer between 0 and 255. Using a Float32Array allows for up to 32 bits of information and gives you more precision but is more resource intensive. This is in contrast to Uint8Array, which is more resource efficient but less precise. This application uses a Uint8Array. A Float32Array or Uint8Array must be created using the keyword new.

In the following code, the Uint8Array is invoked with a single argument that determines the number of indexes it will have by using analyzer.frequencyBinCount.

```
let frequencyData = new Uint8Array(analyzer.frequencyBinCount);
console.log(frequencyData.length); // 1024
```

You now store the frequency domain data in the array using getByteFrequencyData().

```
analyzer.getByteFrequencyData(frequencyData);
```

If the frequencyData array is a Float32Array instead of a Uint8Array, you use the getFloatFrequencyData() method and the code looks like this:

```
analyzer.getFloatFrequencyData(frequencyData);
```

▋ How to *Think About* the `frequencyData` Array

Each index value of the `frequencyData` array can be any number between 0 and 255. This value is correlated with the energy intensity of the frequency band that is designated by that particular array index. The following diagrams can help to clarify this.

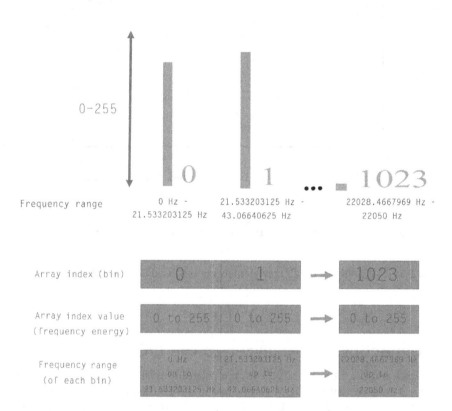

▋ Building the Display Interface

The following line of code renders the current number of bins to the Document Object Model (DOM).

```
$(".bin-count-number").text(analyzer.fftSize / 2); //____Bin count
```

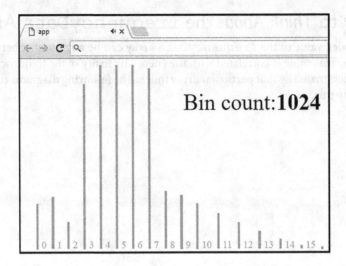

The following for loop creates a div for each bin. Inside each div, a span is created that displays a number that corresponds to each bin.

```
for (let i = 0; i < analyzer.frequencyBinCount; i++) {
  $(".app").append("<div></div> <span>" + i + "</span>");
}
```

The bars variable selects all div elements and is used later in the code.

```
bars = $(".app > div");
```

▐ Connecting the Analyzer to the DOM

To read and use frequencyData, the program must continuously check its current state so that the DOM can be updated with the new information. This can be done by placing analyzer.getByteFrequencyData(frequency Data) in the requestAnimationFrame function. requestAnimation-Frame is a method that tells the browser that you wish to perform an animation. When it is time to update the animation, requestAnimationFrame calls the function that you passed to it. The update rate matches the display refresh rate of the web browser.

```
function update() {
  requestAnimationFrame(update);
  analyzer.getByteFrequencyData(frequencyData);
}
update();
```

To create the vertical frequency bars, the for loop updates the CSS height property of each div stored in the bar variable. The value given to each div is a pixel representation of the current `frequencyData` array index. This value is between 0 and 255 pixels.

```
function update() {
  requestAnimationFrame(update);
  analyzer.getByteFrequencyData(frequencyData);
  for (let i = 0; i < bars.length; i += 1) {
    bars[i].style.height = frequencyData[i] + 'px';
  }
}
update();
```

The user interface of the spectrum analyzer is designed to create a div for *all* bins. You can change the size of the FFT to lower the bin count.

```
analyzer.fftSize = 64;
```

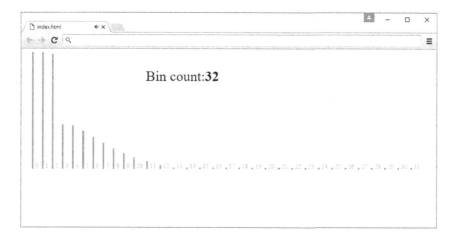

The application you created in this chapter works with frequency-domain data. If you want to work with time-domain data, the `Analyser` node has two methods that let you copy it to a typed array. The first method is `getByteTimeDomainData ()` and is for use with a `Uint8Array()`. The second method is `getFloatTimeDomainData ()` and is for use with `Float32Array()`. To store the time domain data in a `Uint8Array()`, you write the following code:

```
let frequencyData = new Uint8Array(analyzer.frequencyBinCount);
analyzer.getByteTimeDomainData(frequencyData);
```

▐█ Summary

In this chapter, you learned about the `Analyser` node and created a frequency spectrum analyzer application. In the next chapter, you will learn how to build an interactive music sequencer.

23 Building a Step Sequencer

Music applications, like sequencers and drum machines, allow users to record, edit, and playback sounds as a collection of organized note arrangements. Due to the nature of the Web Audio API and its relationship to the DOM, music sequencing applications are a challenge to create. In this chapter, you will learn why this is so and how to meet the challenge by building a basic drum pattern step sequencer.

▌ The Problem

The Web Audio API lets you schedule events immediately or in the future. A problem with this approach is that once an event is scheduled, it cannot be unscheduled. So for example, the following code schedules three drum sounds to play in an eighth note pattern for four bars.

```
let sounds = audioBatchLoader({
    kick:"sounds/kick.mp3",
    snare:"sounds/snare.mp3",
    hihat:"sounds/hihat.mp3"
});

let tempo = 120; //_____BPM (beats per minute)
let eighthNoteTime = (60 / tempo) / 2;
```

DOI: 10.1201/9781003201496-23

```
function playDrums() {
  // Play 4 bars of the following:
  for (let bar = 0; bar < 4; bar++) {
    let time = bar * 8 * eighthNoteTime;
    // Play the bass (kick) drum on beats 1, 5
    sounds.kick.play(time);
    sounds.kick.play(time + 4 * eighthNoteTime);
    // Play the snare drum on beats 3, 7
    sounds.snare.play(time + 2 * eighthNoteTime);
    sounds.snare.play(time + 6 * eighthNoteTime);
    // Play the hi-hat every eighth note.
    for (let i = 0; i < 8; ++i) {
      sounds.hihat.play(time + i * eighthNoteTime);
    }
  }
}
window.onclick = function(event) {
  playDrums();
}
```

If you want to change the tempo relationship of these sounds in the middle of the four bars, you can't. Instead, you have to wait until the sounds have completed playing. This is true of any scheduled events that you might want to change during playback. And this restriction is not relegated to just tempo changes.

■ Can I Use `setInterval` or `setTimeout`?

You might be wondering if you can use `setInterval` or `setTimeout` to solve this problem. The following code uses `setInterval` to increment a counter at a specified beats per minute (BPM), and depending on the counter value, a particular drum sound is played. This creates a rhythmic pattern.

```
let sounds = audioBatchLoader({
    kick: "sounds/kick.mp3",
    snare: "sounds/snare.mp3",
    hihat: "sounds/hihat.mp3"
});

let tempo = 120, //_____BPM (beats per minute)
    milliseconds = 1000,
    eighthNoteTime = ((60 * milliseconds) / tempo) / 2,
    counter = 1;

function playSequence() {
    window.setInterval(function() {
        if (counter === 8) {
            counter = 1;
        } else {
            counter += 1;
        }
        if (counter) {
            sounds.hihat.play();
        }
        if (counter === 3 || counter === 7) {
```

```
      sounds.snare.play();
    }
    if (counter === 1 || counter === 5) {
      sounds.kick.play();
    }
  }, eighthNoteTime);
}
window.onclick = function(event) {
  playSequence();
}
```

The problem with this approach is that both the `setTimeout` and `setInterval` methods have timings that are imprecise and unstable. There are two reasons for this. The first is that the smallest unit of time available to these methods is an integer of 1 millisecond, which is not precise enough for audio sample-level values like 44.100 kHz. The other problem is that unlike the Web Audio API timing clock, these methods can be interrupted by ancillary browser activity like page rendering and redraws. Although you might expect `setInterval` or `setTimeout` to run at every *n*th millisecond, depending on factors outside your control, the value will likely be larger and audibly noticeable.

▐ The Solution

The solution to the problem is to create a relationship between the Web Audio API timing clock and the browser's internal `setTimeout` method to create a *look-ahead* mechanism that recursively loops and checks if events *will be* scheduled at some time in the future. If this is the case, the scheduling happens and the event(s) takes place. This gives you enough leeway to cancel events at the last moment if needed.

One thing to keep in mind is that because `setTimeout` is inherently unstable, we know that this relationship will always have an unstable aspect to it. Whether or not this approach is stable enough for your applications is for you to decide. One thing we can be certain of is that it is much more accurate than using `setInterval` or `setTimeout` on its own.

▐ How It Works

The basis for the relationship between the Web Audio API timing clock and the browser's internal `setTimeout` method is expressed in the following code:

```
let audioContext = new AudioContext();
let futureTickTime = audioContext.currentTime;
function scheduler() {
  if (futureTickTime < audioContext.currentTime + 0.1) {
    futureTickTime += 0.5; /*_can be any time value. 0.5 happens to
be a quarter note at 120 bpm */
    console.log(futureTickTime);
  }
  window.setTimeout(scheduler, 0);
}
```

```
window.onclick = function(){
    audioContext = new AudioContext();
    futureTickTime = audioContext.currentTime;
    scheduler();
}
```

The way the previous code works is that the setTimeout function loops recursively, and upon each iteration, a conditional checks whether the value of futureTickTime is within a tenth of a second of the audioContext.currentTime. If this evaluates to true then futureTickTime is incremented by 0.5, which is *half a second* in "Web Audio Time". The futureTickTime variable remains set at this value until audioContext.currentTime "catches up with it" once again. Then within a tenth of a second, futureTickTime is incremented by a half-second into the future. This pattern continues for as long as the function is allowed to run.

Because a half-second translates to a quarter note at 120 BPM, the following code uses this information to create a 1/4th note timing count that is logged to the console.

```
let audioContext
let futureTickTime;
let counter = 1;
function scheduler() {
    if (futureTickTime < audioContext.currentTime + 0.1) {
        futureTickTime += 0.5; /*_can be any time
value. 0.5 happens to be a quarter note at 120 bpm */
        console.log("This is beat: " + counter);
        counter += 1;
        if (counter > 4) {
            counter = 1;
        }
    }
    window.setTimeout(scheduler, 0);
}

window.onclick = function () {
    audioContext = new AudioContext();
    futureTickTime = audioContext.currentTime;
    scheduler();
}
```

The following code builds on the previous example and plays an oscillator on each count. The oscillator is connected to a gain node named metronome which is connected to the destination. The gain node is added because the final application in this chapter uses it to toggle the oscillator volume on and off.

```
let audioContext,
    futureTickTime,
    counter = 1,
    metronome,
    osc;

function playMetronome(time) {
    let osc = audioContext.createOscillator();
    osc.connect(metronome);
    metronome.connect(audioContext.destination);
    osc.start(time);
    osc.stop(time + 0.1);
}

function scheduler() {
    if (futureTickTime < audioContext.currentTime + 0.1) {
        playMetronome(futureTickTime);
        futureTickTime += 0.5; /*_can be any time
value. 0.5 happens to be a quarter note at 120 bpm */
        console.log("This is beat: " + counter);


        counter += 1;
        if (counter > 4) {
            counter = 1;
        }
    }
    window.setTimeout(scheduler, 0);
}

window.onclick = function () {
    audioContext = new AudioContext();
    futureTickTime = audioContext.currentTime;
```

```
        osc = audioContext.createOscillator();
        metronome = audioContext.createGain();
        scheduler();
}
```

▌ Changing Tempo

If you want to change the tempo, you have to change the time relationship
between events. You can do this by altering when events are scheduled to start
with the futureTickTime variable. The following formula is useful for con-
verting beats (quarter notes) to seconds:

```
let tempo = 120.0; // tempo (in beats per minute);
let secondsPerBeat = (60.0 / tempo);
```

The application you build assumes the use of a 16th note grid. You can design
it with any beat division(s) you want, but for simplicity it is hard-coded with 16
notes. The following code converts the futureTickTime variable from a time
value that represents a quarter note to a time value that represents a 16th note.
The oscillator is also modified to play a different frequency on the downbeat.

```
"use strict";

let audioContext,
    futureTickTime,
    counter = 1,
    metronome,
    tempo = 90,
    secondsPerBeat = 60 / tempo,
    counterTimeValue = (secondsPerBeat / 4),
    oscFrequency = 100,
    osc;

function playMetronome(time) {
    let osc = audioContext.createOscillator();
    if (counter === 1) {
        oscFrequency = 400;
    } else {
        oscFrequency = 100;
    }

    osc.connect(audioContext.destination);
    osc.frequency.value = oscFrequency;
    osc.start(time);
    osc.stop(time + 0.1);
}


function scheduler() {
    if (futureTickTime < audioContext.currentTime + 0.1) {
        playMetronome(futureTickTime);
        futureTickTime += counterTimeValue;
        console.log("This is beat: " + counter);
```

```
            counter += 1;
            if (counter > 16) {
                counter = 1;
            }
        }
    window.setTimeout(scheduler, 0);


}



window.onclick = function () {
    audioContext = new AudioContext();
    futureTickTime = audioContext.currentTime;
    osc = audioContext.createOscillator();
    metronome = audioContext.createGain();
    scheduler();


}
```

You can now change the tempo by modifying the tempo variable.

▌ Building the Sequencer

You are now going to build the sequencer application. Create a copy of the *Web Audio template* folder you created in Chapter 1 and rename it to *sequencer*. In the *index.html* file, reference both the JQuery library and the *audiolib.js* file that you created in the previous chapters.

```
<!DOCTYPE html>
<html>
<head>
<meta charset="UTF-8">
<title>app</title>
<script src="https://ajax.googleapis.com/ajax/libs/jquery/3.6.0/
jquery.min.js"></script>
<script src="js/audiolib.js"></script>
<script src="js/app.js"></script>
<link rel="stylesheet" href="css/app.css">
</head>
<!--_____BEGIN APP-->
<body>

</body>
<!--_____END APP-->
</html>
```

Inside the sequencer folder, create a folder named *sounds* and place audio files for the sequencer application in it (you will need a hihat.mp3, kick.mp3, shaker.mp3, and snare.mp3).

Copy the following code to *app.js* and save the file. This code refactors the previous code you have written. This version is more readable and the metronome is given its own function.

```javascript
"use strict";

  let futureTickTime,
  counter = 1,
  metronome,
  tempo = 90,
  secondsPerBeat = 60 / tempo,
  counterTimeValue = (secondsPerBeat / 4),
  oscFrequency = 100,
  osc;

function playMetronome(time, playing) {
  if (playing) {
    osc = audioContext.createOscillator();
    osc.connect(audioContext.destination);
    if (counter === 1) {
      osc.frequency.value = 500;
    } else {
      osc.frequency.value = 300;

    }

    osc.connect(audioContext.destination);
    osc.start(time);
    osc.stop(time + 0.1);

  }

}

function playTick() {
  console.log("This is 16th note: " + counter);
  counter += 1;
  futureTickTime += counterTimeValue;
  if (counter > 16) {
    counter = 1;

  }

}

function scheduler() {
  if (futureTickTime < audioContext.currentTime + 0.1) {
    playMetronome(futureTickTime, true);
    playTick();

  }

  window.setTimeout(scheduler, 0);

}
```

```
window.onclick = function() {
  futureTickTime = audioContext.currentTime;
  osc = audioContext.createOscillator();
  metronome = audioContext.createGain();
  scheduler();

}
```

■ Playing Back Sounds in Sequence

You will now create a series of arrays that represent music sequencer *tracks*. Each of these arrays stores counter values. On each iteration of the counter, a *for* loop runs to check if any of the arrays holds the current counter value. If any of them does, the sound associated with that array plays. The arrays are associated with the correct sound through a function named scheduleSound(). This function takes four arguments:

- The track array

- The sound to play

- The current count value

- The time to schedule the sound

The track arrays are populated with values so that you can hear a drum sequence immediately.

```
"use strict";

let futureTickTime,
  counter = 1,
  metronome,
  metronomeVolume = 1,
  tempo = 90,
  secondsPerBeat = 60 / tempo,
  counterTimeValue = (secondsPerBeat / 4),
  oscFrequency = 100,
  osc;

/*_____BEGIN load
sounds BOLD */

let sounds = audioBatchLoader({
  kick: "sounds/kick.mp3",
  snare: "sounds/snare.mp3",
  hihat: "sounds/hihat.mp3",
  shaker: "sounds/shaker.mp3"
});

//_____END load sounds */
//_____BEGIN Array Tracks
```

```
let kickTrack = [1, 9, 11],
  snareTrack = [5, 13],
  hiHatTrack = [13, 14, 15, 16],
  shakerTrack = [1, 2, 3, 4, 5, 6, 7, 8, 9, 10, 11, 12, 13, 14, 15,
16];
//_____END Array Tracks
function scheduleSound(trackArray, sound, count, time) {
  for (let i = 0; i < trackArray.length; i += 1) {
    if (count === trackArray[i]) {
      sound.play(time);
    }
  }
}


function playMetronome(time, playing) {
  if (playing) {
    osc = audioContext.createOscillator();
    osc.connect(metronome);
    metronome.gain.value = metronomeVolume;
    metronome.connect(audioContext.destination);

    if (counter === 1) {
      osc.frequency.value = 500;
    } else {
      osc.frequency.value = 300;
    }

    osc.connect(metronome);
    metronome.connect(audioContext.destination);
    osc.start(time);
    osc.stop(time + 0.1);
  }
}


function playTick() {
  console.log("This is 16th note: " + counter);
  counter += 1;
  futureTickTime += counterTimeValue;
  if (counter > 16) {
    counter = 1;
  }
}

function scheduler() {
  if (futureTickTime < audioContext.currentTime + 0.1) {
    playMetronome(futureTickTime, true);
    scheduleSound(kickTrack, sounds.kick, counter, futureTickTime
- audioContext.currentTime);
    scheduleSound(snareTrack, sounds.snare, counter, futureTickTime
- audioContext.currentTime);
    scheduleSound(hiHatTrack, sounds.hihat, counter, futureTickTime
- audioContext.currentTime);
    scheduleSound(shakerTrack, sounds.shaker, counter,
futureTickTime - audioContext.currentTime);
    playTick();
  }
```

```
  window.setTimeout(scheduler, 0);

}
window.onclick = function() {
  futureTickTime = audioContext.currentTime;
  osc = audioContext.createOscillator();
  metronome = audioContext.createGain();
  scheduler();

}
```

You might be wondering why the `scheduleSound()` function invocations are subtracting the `audioContext.currentTime` from the `futureTickTime()`

```
scheduleSound(kickTrack, kickTrack, counter, futureTickTime -
  audioContext.currentTime);
```

This is done because the audio library you built in Chapter 13 is designed to reference `audioContext.currentTime` by default and adds any additional numeric arguments to this value. You subtract `audioContext.current-Time` from `futureTickTime` because these values will be combined when the `play()` method of your library is invoked.

When `scheduler()` is invoked, the drum sequence does not start immediately because it takes time for the audio buffers and files to load thus an event listener invokes the scheduler function when the user clicks the page. In our app, we will change this so that the scheduler is initiated by a *play/stop* button. In your HTML code, create a button with a class of `play-stop-button` and give it the text of `play/stop`.

```
<!DOCTYPE html>
<html>
<head>
<meta charset="UTF-8">
<title>app</title>
        <script src="https://ajax.googleapis.com/ajax/libs/
jquery/3.6.0/jquery.min.js"></script>
<script src="js/audiolib.js"></script>
<script src="js/app.js"></script>
<link rel="stylesheet" href="css/app.css">
</head>
<!--_____BEGIN APP-->
<body>

  <!--HTML code-->
        <button class="play-stop-button">
        Play / Stop
        </button>

</body>
<!--_____END APP-->
</html>
```

You now use JQuery to interface with the DOM and have to wrap your code in a document-ready function. The following code defines the *play/stop* button functionality.

```
"use strict";

$(function() {

  let futureTickTime,
    counter = 1,
    metronome,
    metronomeVolume = 1,
    tempo = 90,
    secondsPerBeat = 60 / tempo,
    counterTimeValue = (secondsPerBeat / 4),
    oscFrequency = 100,
    timerID,
    isPlaying = false,
    osc;

  /*_____BEGIN load
sounds*/

  let sounds = audioBatchLoader({
    kick: "sounds/kick.mp3",
    snare: "sounds/snare.mp3",
    hihat: "sounds/hihat.mp3",
    shaker: "sounds/shaker.mp3"

  });


  //_____END load sounds */

  //_____BEGIN Array Tracks

  let kickTrack = [1, 9, 11],
    snareTrack = [5, 13],
    hiHatTrack = [13, 14, 15, 16],
    shakerTrack = [1, 2, 3, 4, 5, 6, 7, 8, 9, 10, 11, 12, 13, 14,
15, 16];
  //_____END Array Tracks


  function scheduleSound(trackArray, sound, count, time) {
    for (let i = 0; i < trackArray.length; i += 1) {
      if (count === trackArray[i]) {
        sound.play(time);
      }
    }
  }

  function playMetronome(time, playing, volume) {

    if (playing) {
```

```
    osc = audioContext.createOscillator();
    osc.connect(metronome);
    metronome.gain.value = volume;
    metronome.connect(audioContext.destination);
    if (counter === 1) {

      osc.frequency.value = 500;

    } else {
      osc.frequency.value = 300;

    }

    osc.connect(metronome);
    metronome.connect(audioContext.destination);
    osc.start(time);
    osc.stop(time + 0.1);

  }

}

function playTick() {
  console.log("This is 16th note:" + counter);
  counter += 1;
  futureTickTime += counterTimeValue;
  if (counter > 16) {
    counter = 1;

  }

}

function scheduler() {

  if (futureTickTime < audioContext.currentTime + 0.1) {
    playMetronome(futureTickTime, true, metronomeVolume);
    scheduleSound(kickTrack, sounds.kick, counter, futureTickTime
- audioContext.currentTime);
    scheduleSound(snareTrack, sounds.snare, counter,
futureTickTime - audioContext.currentTime);
    scheduleSound(hiHatTrack, sounds.hihat, counter,
futureTickTime - audioContext.currentTime);
    scheduleSound(shakerTrack, sounds.shaker, counter,
futureTickTime - audioContext.currentTime);
    playTick();

  }

  timerID = window.setTimeout(scheduler, 0);

}

function play() {
  osc = audioContext.createOscillator();
  metronome = audioContext.createGain();
  isPlaying = !isPlaying;
```

```
if (isPlaying) {
  counter = 1;
  futureTickTime = audioContext.currentTime;
  scheduler();
} else {
  window.clearTimeout(timerID);

}

}

$(".play-stop-button").on("click", function() {

  play();

});

});
```

If you launch this code from your server and click the *play/start* button, it will start and stop the application.

▮ Creating the User Interface Grid

So far you have built a working 16th note sequencer that plays back sound sequences via a collection of "array tracks" in code. You are now going to create a user interface that allows users to create these sequences from a web page.

To do this, you create four div elements positioned as rows, and each of these contains 16 child divs. The CSS displays these child divs horizontally as a collection of small squares. The first row controls playback of the kick drum, the second row the snare, the third row the hi-hat, and the fourth row the shaker. The sequencer has an additional button that turns the metronome on and off and an input slider that controls the tempo.

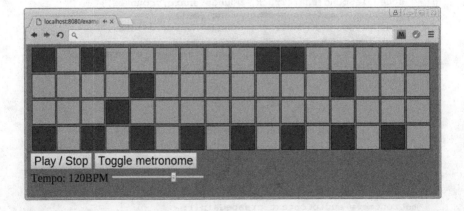

◼ HTML

The following code is the HTML for the application:

```html
<!DOCTYPE html>
<html>
  <head>
    <meta charset="UTF-8">
    <title>app</title>
    <script src="https://ajax.googleapis.com/ajax/libs/jquery/3.6.0/
jquery.min.js"></script>
    <script src="js/audiolib.js"></script>
    <script src="js/app.js"></script>
    <link rel="stylesheet" href="css/app.css">
  </head>
  <!--_____BEGIN APP-->
  <body>
    <div class="app-grid">
    </div>
    <button class="play-stop-button">
    Play / Stop
    </button>
    <button class="metronome">Toggle metronome</button>
    <div id="tempoBox">Tempo: <span id="showTempo">120</span>BPM
      <input id="tempo" type="range" min="30.0" max="160.0"
      step="1" value="120" ></div>

  </body>
  <!--_____END APP-->
</html>
```

◼ CSS

The following code is the CSS for the application:

```css
body{
  background-color:red;
  font-size:25px;
}
button{
  margin-bottom:5px;
  font-size:25px;
}
.track-step{
  width:50px;
  height:50px;
  display:inline-block;
  background-color:orange;
  outline-style:solid;
  outline-width:1px;
  margin-left:5px;
}
```

To create the `div` elements for the grid, you use a nested JavaScript for loop. Each collection of grid items has a parent container. Type the following for-loop at the very bottom of your JQuery code.

```
$(function(){
 // …. previous app code

    //_____BEGIN create grid
    for (let i=1; i <= 4; i += 1) {
        $(".app-grid").append("<div
class='track-" + i + "-container' </div>");
        for (let j=1; j < 17; j += 1) {
            $(".track-" + i + "-container").append("<div
class='grid-item track-step step-" + j + "'</div>");
        }
    }
    //_____END create grid

});
```

The following code allows you to toggle the metronome on and off:

```
$(function(){
    // …..... previous app code

    $(".play-stop-button").on("click", function() {
        play();
    });

    //_____BEGIN metronome toggle
    $(".metronome").on("click", function() {
        if(metronomeVolume){
            metronomeVolume = 0;
        }else{
            metronomeVolume = 1;
        }
    });
    //_____END metronome toggle

    //_____BEGIN create grid
    for (let i=1; i <= 4; i += 1) {
        $(".app-grid").append("<div
class='track-" + i + "-container' </div>");
        for (let j=1; j < 17; j += 1) {
            $(".track-" + i + "-container").append("<div class='grid-
item track-step step-" + j + "'</div>");
        }
    }
    //_____END create grid

});
```

Next, you write code that lets users control the tempo from the HTML input range slider and displays the current tempo on the web page. First, modify the `playTick()` function:

```
function playTick() {
  secondsPerBeat = 60 / tempo;
  counterTimeValue = (secondsPerBeat / 4);
  console.log("This is 16th note: " + counter);
  counter += 1;
  futureTickTime += counterTimeValue;
  if (counter > 16) {
    counter = 1;
  }
}
```

Then create the event listener used to control the tempo from the slider:

```
$(".metronome").on("click", function() {
  if (metronomeVolume.gain.value) {
    metronomeVolume.gain.value = 0;
  } else {
    metronomeVolume.gain.value = 1;
  }
});
$("#tempo").on("change", function() {
  tempo = $(this).val();
  $("#showTempo").html(tempo);
});
```

You can now modify the tempo of the sequence by moving the HTML input slider.

▌ Adding Interactivity to the Grid Elements

Each collection of elements with a class of grid-item has a parent. The parent elements are dynamically created as shown in the following code:

```
<div class="track-1-container"></div>
<div class="track-2-container"></div>
<div class="track-3-container"></div>
<div class="track-4-container"></div>
```

JQuery has a method named index() that allows you to capture an element's index value relative to a parent element. In the case of the sequencer application, the index value of the first grid-item of each row is 0 and the last grid-item index is 15. You can give this value an offset of +1 so that the first index grid-item is referenced as 1 and the last is referenced as 16. This allows for a correlation between the grid-item index values and the counter value. You can capture this information by setting an event listener to all elements with a class of grid-item. When the user clicks the grid-item, the offset index value is either *pushed to* or *removed from* a corresponding track array dependent on whether the grid-item is *active or not*. This is what determines if a sound will play at a certain point in the music sequence. The following code implements this feature and also modifies the CSS background-color of the grid-item based on whether it is active or not.

```
//_____BEGIN create grid
for (var i = 1; i <= 4; i += 1) {
  $(".app-grid").append("<div class='track-" + i + "-container'</
div>");
  for (var j = 1; j < 17; j += 1) {
    $(".track-" + i + "-container").append("<div class='grid-item
    track-step step-" + j + "'</div>");
  }
}
//_____END create grid
//_____BEGIN Grid interactivity
  function sequenceGridToggler(domEle, arr) {
    $(domEle).on("mousedown", ".grid-item", function() {
      var gridIndexValue = $(this).index(); /*_____Get index
        of grid-item*/
      var offset = gridIndexValue + 1; /*_____Add +1 so
        value starts at 1 instead of 0*/
      var index = arr.indexOf(offset); /*_____Check if
        value exists in array*/
      if (index > -1) { /*_____If index of
        item exist.....*/
        arr.splice(index, 1); //_____then remove
it....
        $(this).css("backgroundColor", ""); /*_____and change
          color of DOM element to default*/
      } else { /*_____If item
does
        not exist.....*/
        arr.push(offset); /*_____then push it
to
        track array*/
        $(this).css("background-color", "purple"); /*_and change
          color of DOM element to purple.*/
      }
    });
  }
  sequenceGridToggler(".track-1-container", kickTrack);
  sequenceGridToggler(".track-2-container", snareTrack);
  sequenceGridToggler(".track-3-container", hiHatTrack);
  sequenceGridToggler(".track-4-container", shakerTrack);
//_____END Grid interactivity
```

Now set the track arrays so that they are empty.

```
let  kickTrack = [1, 9, 11],
     snareTrack = [5, 13],
     hiHatTrack = [13, 14, 15, 16],
     shakerTrack = [1, 2, 3, 4, 5, 6, 7, 8, 9, 10, 11, 12, 13,
        14, 15, 16];
let kickTrack = [ ],
    snareTrack = [ ],
    hiHatTrack = [ ],
    shakerTrack = [ ];
```

You can now run the sequencer and playback sounds by clicking the squares. The tempo also changes when the slider is moved.

▌ Summary

In this chapter, you learned how to build a basic music sequencer. You now understand the core techniques needed to build Web Audio API applications that rely on event scheduling.

24 AJAX and JSON

In this chapter, you are going to learn how to query data using web APIs and to create your own web API for accessing synth patch data to use in a web audio synthesizer. Third-party web services commonly allow a portion of their data to be accessible via a web API. This gives you the ability to query data on their server and use their data in your applications. An example is the iTunes public search API that lets developers search media titles in the iTunes store. To begin, you must first learn about two technologies: AJAX and JSON.

■ AJAX

AJAX is an acronym that stands for *Asynchronous JavaScript and XML*. This is a technology that allows you to use JavaScript to make network requests and access data asynchronously. You have already worked with AJAX in previous chapters when loading audio buffers using the XMLHttpRequest object and the fetch API. The X in AJAX refers to XML, which stands for Extensible Markup Language. This was originally the data exchange format used with AJAX and is rarely used now. In modern web development, the data exchange format you use is JSON.

DOI: 10.1201/9781003201496-24

▮ JSON

JSON stands for *JavaScript Object Notation*, and it is a data exchange format for transmitting and receiving data over the HTTP protocol when working with web APIs. JSON objects are nearly identical to JavaScript object literals, making them easy to work with. The difference between a JSON object and a JavaScript object literal is that JSON objects are not assigned to a variable and their keys need to be explicitly written as strings. JSON objects are stored in JavaScript files. The following code is an example of a JSON object:

```
{
  "buzzFunk": [{
    "type": "sawtooth",
    "frequency": 65.25
  }, {
    "type": "triangle",
    "frequency": 65.25
  }, {
    "type": "sawtooth",
    "frequency": 67.25
  }]
}
```

▮ Making an AJAX Call to the iTunes Search API

To demonstrate how to interact with a third-party web API, you are now going to make a query to the iTunes search API.

Make a copy of the "web audio template" folder you created in Chapter 1, rename it to "itunes api example" and drag it to the sidebar in Sublime Text. Next, copy the following code to the app.js file:

```
fetch("https://itunes.apple.com/search?term=funk&media=music&callb
ack")
.then(response => response.json())
.then(data => console.log(data))
```

Go to Start Sublime Server and in your web browser go to localhost:8080. Open the console and you will see an object being returned.

If you click the arrow and unfold the object, you will see a list of objects that each contains data.

You have just queried the iTunes search API for any music that includes the keyword "funk" and are now in possession of a JavaScript object that contains this data.

▋ How the Code Works

The fetch function is an abstraction of the XMLHttpRequest object that lets developers make AJAX requests with a simple syntax. Fetch issues a request to a server that returns the queried data. The first argument of fetch is a URL (commonly referred to as an endpoint). The endpoint is written as a string, and if you look closely, you can see the search terms embedded in it. These are key/value pairs such as term=funk and media=music.

```
"https://itunes.apple.com/search?term=funk&media=music";
```

The part of the endpoint after the "?" symbol is called the *query string*. This part of the URL contains the data that is being queried. The "&" symbol separates the key/value pairs.

The iTunes API search terms are assigned to specific keys and in the previous code, these are term and media. There is no standardization across web APIs for key/value names, and they are different for each web API. Because the URL structure for all web APIs is different, you will need to read the documentation for any that you are working with. The documentation for the iTunes search API is here: https://affiliate.itunes.apple.com/resources/documentation/itunes-store-web-service-search-api/.

The fetch API encapsulates callbacks inside a method named then. The first callback returns the response data and, in our example, converts it to JSON format. The second callback is used to log the data to the console.

```
fetch("https://itunes.apple.com/search?term=funk&media=music")
  .then(response => response.json())   // Convert response to JSON
  .then(data => console.log(data));    // Logs data to console
```

▮ Creating Your Own Web API to Reference Synthesizer Patch Data

You are now going to create your own web API. The goal of this exercise is to demonstrate how to create a very basic web API using a JSON object that contains synthesizer patch data. The data you will create for your web API is a collection of settings for the oscillators of a synth. The user interface of the application appears as in the figure below. The completed code is available in the resource examples for this chapter.

▮ Node.js

The JavaScript that you've written up to this point has been limited to the context of a web browser. Node.JS is a downloadable program that lets you run JavaScript directly from the terminal on your computer. The terminal is a built-in application that gives you access to the internal data of your *entire* computer. Node.Js lets you write JavaScript in the terminal to manipulate files on your computer as well as create and launch scripts, build web servers, and perform other actions. In our case, we are going to use Node.JS to create a very basic web API that contains synthesizer patch data.

To get started, you must first download and install Node.js. You can do so by going to the following URL and following the directions for your operating system. https://nodejs.org/en/.

Once the application is done installing it will require terminal access. Windows OS terminal commands are slightly different than on Mac and Linux systems. If you are using Windows OS, we suggest that you download a program called Git Bash and substitute it for the Windows OS terminal. Git Bash lets you use Unix and Linux commands on Windows OS and allows for a simpler experience.

To download and install Git Bash go to this URL: https://gitforwindows.org/.

■ Launching the Terminal

On Windows OS open Git Bash from your applications list.

On a Mac OS, the terminal is accessible via the Application folder.

On Linux OS, the terminal is called *terminal* and is available where other applications are located depending on your version of Linux.

■ Launching Node.JS

To check if Node.JS is installed correctly, launch your computer's terminal and type the word "node" into the prompt and press enter on your keyboard. If you get a command saying command not recognized then NodeJS was not installed. Otherwise, it is installed. Feel free to experiment by typing JavaScript statements into the prompt such as 1 + 1. You execute your code by pressing the enter key.

■ Getting Started

On your desktop (or another directory of your choice) create a folder named server.

Open your terminal and type the command cd. The cd command stands for current directory and lets you navigate between directories in the terminal. After you type the letters cd, drag the app folder to the terminal. Dragging a folder to the terminal is a way to reference its directory location without manually typing it out. Press enter on your keyboard.

In the terminal type npm init and press enter. You are presented with a prompt that says "This utility will walk you through creating a package.json file". You are then asked a question as to the name of your application. You can either type a name or press enter to provide a default answer and immediately skip to the next question. Providing custom answers to any of the questions is not required to create the application.

Once all prompted questions are complete a file named package.json will appear in the server directory. This file contains default values for the application you are creating.

■ Node.JS Hello World

Before we build the application let's first demonstrate how to run JavaScript files using Node.JS. In your server folder create a file named app.js and type this basic JavaScript function into the file.

```
function textContent(data){
    return data;
}
console.log(textContent("Hello World"));
```

Before we run the code, our terminal must be referencing the directory of app.js. Open your terminal and go to the directory of your server folder by typing cd, and then dragging the folder named server to the terminal. When you're done, press enter. To run the app.js file using Node.Js, you type the name of the file prefaced with the node command as shown below.

```
node app.js
```

In the terminal, the string "Hello World" is displayed. When you are done open app.js in your code editor, delete the code you wrote, and save the file.

■ Building a Simple Web API

Node.JS has a collection of built-in tools (also called modules) that let you manipulate files, work with network requests and do various other tasks. One of these modules is named http and it is used to create web servers. To use the http module, you must first import it into your application. There are two different ways to import modules into Node.JS. You can either use a built-in function named require or use the JavaScript import statement. The import statement is standardized as part of the ES6 version of JavaScript but at the time of this writing, it is not implemented in most JavaScript environments. Node.JS lets you use the import statement as an experimental feature. For our purposes, we will use the import statement due to its standardization in the JavaScript specification.

Go to your applications package.json file and in the JSON object type: "type": "module".

The contents of package.json now look similar to this example:

```
{
  "name": "app",
  "version": "1.0.0",
  "description": "",
  "type": "module",
  "main":"index.js",
  "scripts": {
    "test": "echo \"Error: no test specified\" && exit 1"
  },

  "author": "",
  "license": "ISC"
}
```

At the top of app.js in your server folder import the http module using this syntax:

```
import http from "http";
```

Now write the following code after the import statement.

```
import http from 'http';
http.createServer(function (req, res) {
    res.write('Hello Sound API!');
    res.end();
}).listen(3000); // server listens at port 3000
console.log("Server listening on port 3000");
```

In the terminal go to the server folder directory and type node app.js. Open your browser and go to localhost:3000. You will see the text "Hello Sound API". To stop the program, select the terminal and press the CTRL and the C keys at the same time.

For our purposes we do not want to write text to the client, we want to respond with a JSON object. Update the previous code in app.js to render a JSON object by replacing it with the code below.

```
import http from 'http';
http.createServer(function (req, res) {
    res.write('Hello Sound API!'); // remove this line
    res.setHeader('Access-Control-Allow-Origin', '*');
    res.setHeader('Content-Type', 'application/json');
    res.end(JSON.stringify({})); // Empty JSON object
}).listen(3000);

console.log("Server listening on port 3000");
```

The previous code when executed renders an *empty* JSON object to the browser. Let's change this and create a JSON object that we intend to use. Update the code in app.js to look like the following example:

```
import http from 'http';
let patches = {
  "buzzFunk": [{
    "type": "sawtooth",
    "frequency": 65.25
  }, {
    "type": "triangle",
    "frequency": 65.25
  }, {
    "type": "sawtooth",
    "frequency": 67.25
  }]
}
http.createServer(function (req, res) {
    res.setHeader('Access-Control-Allow-Origin', '*');
    res.setHeader('Content-Type', 'application/json');
    res.end(JSON.stringify(patches)); // non-empty object
}).listen(3000);
console.log("Server listening on port 3000");
```

In your terminal, launch the Node.JS server.

```
node app.js
```

In your browser go to localhost:3000 to see the object rendered.

How the Code Works

The http object has a method named `createServer` that takes a callback. The callback has two augments that are both objects. The first argument is named request (abbreviated as req) and the second is named response (abbreviated as res). The request object contains methods that *create* server requests *from* your Node.JS application. The response object contains methods that *respond* to http requests made *to* your application. For our application, we use two methods of the response object and these are `setHeader` and `end`.

Http headers are additional information that is transferred during an http request or response. In our code, the `setHeader` method is invoked twice. The first instance enables a mode called CORS. CORS stands for Cross Origin Resource Sharing and it is a mechanism that determines if a web server will allow or restrict access to resources (such as JSON objects). For example, if your browser is rendering *yourwebsite.com* and you make an AJAX request to retrieve a JSON object from *mywebsite.com*, you will get an error *unless* the server hosting mywebsite.com is programmed to enable the shared resource via CORS.

For more information on CORS see this URL: https://developer.mozilla.org/en-US/docs/Web/HTTP/CORS.

In our case, by default the server rejects AJAX requests, therefore, we must enable CORS to change that and we use the following code to do so:

```
res.setHeader('Access-Control-Allow-Origin', '*');    // CORS
enabled
```

The setHeader method also sets the type of content we are sending. In this case, it is JSON.

```
res.setHeader('Content-Type', 'application/json');
```

The res.end method is used to end the response process and, in our case, return a JSON object to the browser. Before being rendered to the browser the JSON object must first be converted to a string and this is done using the stringify method.

```
res.end(JSON.stringify(patches));
```

You now have working server-side JSON code available for a basic web API. You will now make a request from a client.

Client Request

On your desktop (or directory of your choice) make a copy of the "web audio template" folder you created in Chapter 1 and rename the folder "web_app". Open the web_app directory in Sublime Text, open the app.js file in the js directory and type the following code:

```
fetch("http://localhost:3000/")      // points to the endpoint of our
web api server
```

```
.then(response => response.json())   // Convert response to JSON
.then(data => console.log(data));    // Logs data to console
```

Save the file.

Start your Node.JS server application per the command node app. Start Sublime Server and point your web browser to localhost:8080. Open the developer tools to view the JSON object in the console. You have successfully retrieved the data from your Node.JS application.

If you unfold the object, you will see its internals.

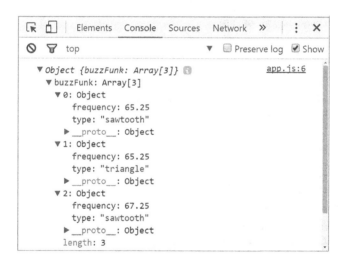

▌ Building a Synth Application to Consume the Data

You will now build a web audio synth to load and playback your patch data.

▌ The Patch Data Explained

The data structure of the JSON object contains properties and each represents a patch name. A patch is a collection of oscillator data that when combined makes a unique sound. The following example has three patches and they are named buzzFunk, gameSound, and zapper. In your Node.JS, app.js file removes the previous patch data and replaces it with the code below.

```
let patches = {
    "buzzFunk": [{            // this is a patch
        "type": "sawtooth",
        "frequency": 65.25,

    }, {
        "type": "triangle",
        "frequency": 65.25,

    }, {

        "type": "sawtooth",
        "frequency": 67.25,
    }],
    "gameSound": [{           // this is a patch
        "type": "square",
        "frequency": 100.25,


    }, {
        "type": "triangle",
        "frequency": 65.25,
    }, {

        "type": "sawtooth",
        "frequency": 67.25,
    }],
    "zapper": [{              // this is a patch
        "type": "square",
        "frequency": 80.25,


    }, {
        "type": "triangle",
        "frequency": 300.25,
    }, {

        "type": "sawtooth",
        "frequency": 40.25,

    }, {

        "type": "sine",
        "frequency": 30.25,
    },
    {

        "type": "sine",
        "frequency": 100.25,

    }]
}
```

Each patch consists of an array containing objects that hold oscillator data. When this data is loaded into your synth, all oscillator data combine to create a single sound for each patch. Each object has `type`, `frequency` settings for the oscillator that references it.

The HTML and CSS code for the keyboard interface is given below. In the web_app directory, copy the HTML code to `index.html` and the CSS code to `app.css`.

▌ HTML

```
<!DOCTYPE html>
<html>

<head>
    <meta charset="UTF-8">
    <title>app</title>
    <script src="https://ajax.googleapis.com/ajax/libs/
jquery/3.6.0/jquery.min.js"></script>
    <script src="js/app.js"></script>
    <link rel="stylesheet" href="css/app.css">
</head>

<!--_____BEGIN APP-->

<body>
    <h1>Synthy API </h1>
    <h3><span>Click here to turn on synth.</span></h3>
    <ul id="piano">
        <li>
            <div class="white-key key" id="c1"></div>
        </li>
        <li>
            <div class="black-key key" id="c#1"></div>
        </li>
        <li>
            <div class="white-key key" id="d1"></div>
        </li>
        <li>
            <div class="black-key key" id="d#1"></div>
        </li>
        <li>
            <div class="white-key key" id="e1"></div>
        </li>
        <li>
            <div class="white-key key" id="f1"></div>
        </li>
        <li>
            <div class="black-key key" id="f#1"></div>
        </li>
        <li>
            <div class="white-key key" id="g1"></div>
        </li>
        <li>
            <div class="black-key key" id="g#1"></div>
```

```
    </li>
    <li>
        <div class="white-key key" id="a1"></div>
    </li>
    <li>
        <div class="black-key key" id="b#1"></div>
    </li>
    <li>
        <div class="white-key key" id="b1"></div>
    </li>
    <li>
        <div class="white-key key" id="c2"></div>
    </li>
    <li>
        <div class="black-key key" id="c#2"></div>
    </li>
    <li>
        <div class="white-key key" id="d2"></div>
    </li>
    <li>
        <div class="black-key key" id="d#2"></div>
    </li>
    <li>
        <div class="white-key key" id="e2"></div>
    </li>
    <li>
        <div class="white-key key" id="f2"></div>
    </li>
    <li>
        <div class="black-key key" id="f#2"></div>
    </li>
    <li>
        <div class="white-key key" id="g2"></div>
    </li>
    <li>
        <div class="black-key key" id="g#2"></div>
    </li>
    <li>
        <div class="white-key key" id="a2"></div>
    </li>
    <li>
        <div class="black-key key" id="b#2"></div>
    </li>
    <li>
        <div class="white-key key" id="b2"></div>
    </li>
    <li>
        <div class="white-key key" id="c3"></div>
    </li>
    <li>
        <div class="black-key key" id="c#3"></div>
    </li>
    <li>
        <div class="white-key key" id="d3"></div>
    </li>
    <li>
        <div class="black-key key" id="d#3"></div>
    </li>
```

```html
        <li>
            <div class="white-key key" id="e3"></div>
        </li>
        <li>
            <div class="white-key key" id="f3"></div>
        </li>
        <li>
            <div class="black-key key" id="f#3"></div>
        </li>
        <li>
            <div class="white-key key" id="g3"></div>
        </li>
        <li>
            <div class="black-key key" id="g#3"></div>
        </li>
        <li>
            <div class="white-key key" id="a3"></div>
        </li>
        <li>
            <div class="black-key key" id="b#3"></div>
        </li>
        <li>
            <div class="white-key key" id="b3"></div>
        </li>
    </ul>
</body>

<!--_____END APP-->

</html>
```

▌ CSS

```css
body{
  background-color:purple;
  width: 100%;
}

h1{
  font-family:"impact";
  color:rgb(228, 208, 230);
  margin-left:5%;
  font-size:70px;

}

h3{
  font-family:"impact";
  color:rgb(228, 208, 230);
  margin-left:5%;
  font-size:30px;
}

li {
  list-style:none;
  float:left;
```

```css
  display:inline;
  width:40px;
  position:relative;
}

.white-key{
  display:block;
  height:220px;
  background:#fff;
  border:1px solid #ddd;
  border-radius:0 0 3px 3px;
}

/* Black keys */
.black-key {
  display:inline-block;
  position:absolute;
  top:0px;
  left:-12px;
  width:25px;
  height:125px;
  background:#000;
  z-index:1;

}
```

Delete any code present in web _ app/js/app.js and replace it with the following code.

```javascript
"use strict";
let synth;

$(function() {
    $(".key").on("mouseover", function() {

        let index = $(this).index('.key');
        synth.play(index);
    });
    $(".key").on("mouseout", function() {
        synth.stop();
    });

    $("h3>span").on("click",function(){
        synth = apiReader("http://localhost:3000", "buzzFunk");    //
JSON loading function
        $(this).text("Synth enabled! Hover over keys to hear sound");
    });
});
```

In your web_app folder, js directory creates a new file named module.js and references it in the index.html file between the JQuery library and app.js file.

```html
< head>
        <link rel="stylesheet" href="css/app.css">
<script src="https://ajax.googleapis.com/ajax/libs/jquery/3.6.0/
jquery.min.js"></script>
```

```
<script src="js/module.js"></script>
<script src="js/app.js"></script>
</head>
```

In module.js, write the following code:

```
"use strict";
const audioContext= new AudioContext();
let apiReader = function(endpoint, patchProp) {

        fetch(endpoint)
            .then(response => response.json())  // Convert response
to JSON
            .then(data => app.patchParams = data[patchProp]);    //
Logs data to console

    let app = {
        patchParams: undefined,
        gainNodes: undefined,
        oscillators: undefined,

        play: function(id) {

            app.oscillators = app.patchParams.map(function(val, i)
{

                let osc = audioContext.createOscillator();
                osc.type=val.type;
                osc.frequency.value=val.frequency;
                osc.detune.value=(val.frequency)+(id*100);
                osc.connect(audioContext.destination);
                osc.start(audioContext.currentTime);
                return osc;
            });
        },
        stop: function() {
            for (let i = 0; i < app.oscillators.length; i += 1) {
                app.oscillators[i].stop(audioContext.currentTime);
            }
        }
    };
    return app;
};
```

Launch the index.html file from Sublime Server, in the browser click the text that says "Click here to turn on synth" and hover your mouse over the synth keys. You will hear the synth play a collection of oscillators that reference the settings of the loaded patch data.

▋ How the Code Works

To enable the synth, the user must first click the text titled "Click here to turn on synth". This event triggers the apiReader to load synth data from our node. js server.

```
let synth;
$(function() {
 // code...

    $("h3>span").on("click",function(){
        synth = apiReader("http://localhost:3000", "zapper");
        $(this).text("Synth enabled! Hover over keys to hear
sound");
    });
});
```

In the `module.js` file, the factory function named `apiReader` takes two arguments. The first argument is named `endpoint` and is the endpoint location of the JSON file. The second argument is named `patchProp` and is the property of the JSON object that contains the synth patch data. The endpoint argument is passed to the fetch function. In the body of the second fetch callback, the selected patch of the returned object is stored as a property of the app object named `app.patchParams`. This is highlighted in the following code example.

```
    fetch(endpoint)
        .then(response => response.json()) // Convert response to
JSON
        .then(data => app.patchParams = data[patchProp]); //
stores data to app.patchParams
```

The `app` object contains the properties and methods that *create, connect, start,* and *stop* oscillators using the selected JSON object data values. The first method of the app object is named `play`. It takes a single argument and is the index value of a DOM element that represents a key. When the `play` method is invoked, the map method loops through each object in the `app.patchParams` array and creates an oscillator on each iteration. The `type`, `frequency.value`, and `detune.value` properties of each oscillator are assigned. Each oscillator is then connected to the node graph and set to start playing.

```
app.oscillators = app.patchParams.map(function(val) {
  let osc = audioContext.createOscillator();
  osc.type = val.type;
  osc.frequency.value = val.frequency;
  osc.detune.value = (val.frequency) + (id * 100);
  osc.connect(audioContext.destination);
  osc.start(audioContext.currentTime);
  return osc;
});
```

The following code provides the index value of a DOM element (the keyboard note the user hovers their mouse over) multiplied by 100. The result is added to the oscillator frequency and assigned to the `detune.value` property. This makes the oscillators playback at half-step intervals relative to the keyboard interface.

```
osc.detune.value = (val.frequency) + (id * 100);
```

Each oscillator is then returned and stored in an array named `app.oscillators`.

The stop method is used to stop the oscillators from playing. This method loops through app.oscillators and invokes a Web Audio API stop method on each one.

```
stop: function() {
  for (let i = 0; i < app.oscillators.length; i += 1) {
    app.oscillators[i].stop(audioContext.currentTime);
  }
}
```

The play and stop methods in web_app/js/module.js are invoked using two event listeners in web_dev/js/app.js. The event listeners start and stop the oscillators on mouse events.

```
$(".key").on("mouseover", function() {
  let index = $(this).index('.key');
  synth.play(index);
});
$(".key").on("mouseout", function() {
  synth.stop();
});
```

When the play method is invoked, the current index value of the div element (the "keyboard note") is captured and passed to the function.

```
let index = $(this).index('.key');//__get index value of key
synth.play(index);//_____pass it to play method
```

▐▌ Extending the API

The code in module.js is designed to load only the type and frequency of oscillators, but what if you wanted to load other custom settings such as volume? The following code adds a volume setting to each oscillator. In the example below, only one patch named "buzzFunk" is updated but feel free to update all patches. Don't forget to restart the server after the code update.

```
{
  "buzzFunk": [{
    "type": "sawtooth",
    "frequency": 65.25,
    "volume": 1
  }, {
    "type": "triangle",
    "frequency": 65.25,
    "volume": 1
  }, {
    "type": "sawtooth",
    "frequency": 67.25,
    "volume": 0.3
  }]
}
```

▌ module.js

```javascript
"use strict";
const audioContext= new AudioContext();
let apiReader = function(endpoint, patchProp) {

    fetch(endpoint)
        .then(response => response.json())  // Convert response
to JSON
        .then(data => app.patchParams = data[patchProp]);   //
Logs data to console

    let app = {
        patchParams: undefined,
        gainNodes: undefined,
        oscillators: undefined,
        play: function(id) {
            app.gainNodes = app.patchParams.map(function(val) {
                let gain = audioContext.createGain();
                gain.gain.value = val.volume;
                return gain;
            });
            app.oscillators = app.patchParams.map(function(val, i)
{

                let osc = audioContext.createOscillator();
                osc.type = val.type;
                osc.frequency.value = val.frequency;
                osc.detune.value = (val.frequency) + (id * 100);
                osc.connect(app.gainNodes[i]);
                app.gainNodes[i].connect(audioContext.destination);
                osc.connect(audioContext.destination); //Remove this line
                osc.start(audioContext.currentTime);

                return osc;
            });
        },

        stop: function() {
            for (let i = 0; i < app.oscillators.length; i += 1) {
                app.oscillators[i].stop(audioContext.currentTime);
            }
        }
    };

    return app;
};
```

These file modifications give your code the ability to create a gain node for
each oscillator. The play method of the app object contains a map method
that creates the gain nodes and sets the gain.gain.value property for
each one. All gain nodes are placed in an array that is assigned to app.
gainNodes.

```
app.gainNodes = app.patchParams.map(function(val) {
  let gain = audioContext.createGain();
  gain.gain.value = val.volume;
  return gain;
});
```

The oscillators are then connected to the gain nodes in the second map method.

```
app.oscillators = app.patchParams.map(function(val, i) {
  let osc = audioContext.createOscillator();
  osc.type = val.type;
  osc.frequency.value = val.frequency;
  osc.detune.value = (val.frequency) + (id * 100);
  osc.connect(app.gainNodes[i]);
  app.gainNodes[i].connect(audioContext.destination);
  osc.start(audioContext.currentTime);
  return osc;
});
```

▌ Summary

In this chapter, you learned how to query third-party web APIs, work with JSON files, and create your own web API to load patch data for a synthesizer. The application you created only begins to explore what is possible. For a challenge, try incorporating filters, LFOs, delays, and other settings. For another challenge, create an HTML form that lets users load patches from the applications UI directly. In the next chapter, you will learn about the future of JavaScript and various resources for continued learning.

25 The Future of JavaScript and the Web Audio API

In this book, you have learned the core concepts behind the JavaScript programming language and the Web Audio API. To keep from overcomplicating things, parts of both the JavaScript language and the Web Audio API have been omitted. This chapter presents some of the areas that were skipped and provides you a few suggestions about what you can learn now to future-proof your new skills.

▮ Web Audio 3D Spacial Positioning

In addition to the `StereoPanner` node, there is one other spacial positioning node called the PannerNode that allows for 3D style panning.

The idea behind 3D spacial positioning is that sound is modified in relation to two objects in a three-dimensional space. The utility of this approach is that the `PannerNode` can be programmed to work with an avatar such as a video game character, where sound that is generated in a "virtual world" is perceived from a first-person perspective. Volume changes take place automatically based on the virtual "distance" between the listener and any sound-generating virtual objects. For added realism, filters, reverberation, and other effects can be programmed to change the characteristics of sound based on the perceived position of virtual objects. You can read about `PannerNode` at the following URL: https://developer.mozilla.org/en-US/docs/Web/API/PannerNode.

▐ Raw Modification of Audio Buffer Data

The Web Audio API allows for the raw modification of audio data. You do this by either creating empty audio buffers and populating them with your own programmed data or by modifying buffers that already contain data such as audio file information. These modifications can be used to create custom effects and other useful things like noise generators. The node used for this is called `AudioWorklet`. You can read about the `AudioWorklet` node at this URL: https://developer.mozilla.org/en-US/docs/Web/API/AudioWorklet.

▐ Suggestions for Continued Learning

JavaScript

JavaScript is always changing and updating. The continued updates for the language are colloquially called ES-Next. A list of continued updates to the language is available here: https://developer.mozilla.org/en-US/docs/Web/JavaScript/Language_Resources.

Node.js

https://nodejs.org

Node.js is a *server-side* JavaScript environment based on V8, which is the same JavaScript engine that runs Google Chrome. Instead of running JavaScript from a web browser, Node.js allows you to run JavaScript from the terminal on your computer. It can be used to automate computer tasks, run web servers, and communicate with databases.

Libraries and Front-End Frameworks

In this book, you learned about a library named JQuery that makes writing DOM code easier. There are other libraries and frameworks that are available to help make your code easy to read and maintain. The most popular front-end library is called React. You can read about React at this URL: https://reactjs.org/.

A front-end framework that I believe is worth your investment of time is called SVELTE.

You can read about SVELTE at this URL: https://svelte.dev/.

The Web MIDI API

https://www.w3.org/TR/webmidi/

MIDI, which stands for Music Instrument Digital Interface, is a digital music instrument protocol created in 1982 by Dave Smith and Chet Wood. The Web MIDI API allows users to control and manipulate MIDI-equipped devices using web browsers.

Open Sound Control

http://opensoundcontrol.org/

According to their website, Open Sound Control (OSC) is "a protocol for communication among computers, sound synthesizers, and other multimedia devices that is optimized for modern networking technology". In other words, OSC is a protocol that facilitates the communication between hardware and software over a network.

▌ Summary

In this chapter, you were presented with a list of options for continued learning. Even though JavaScript has been taught here in the context of working with audio, it is important to keep in mind that programming is a useful cross-disciplinary skill that you can use to solve many different types of problems.

▌ Further Reading

- JavaScript: The Definitive Guide by David Flanagan.

- Website of Nicholas C. Zakas: https://humanwhocodes.com/.

- Multithreaded JavaScript. Concurrency Beyond the Event Loop by Thomas Hunter II and Bryan English.

- You Don't Know JS Book Series by Kyle Simpson.

▌ Book Website

http://javascriptforsoundartists.com

Index

Printed in the United States
by Baker & Taylor Publisher Services